Fort Gibson Historic Site, Fort Gibson, Oklahoma.
(Photo by the author)

A TRAIL OF TEARS

The American Indian in the Civil War

Rex T. Jackson

HERITAGE BOOKS
2007

HERITAGE BOOKS

AN IMPRINT OF HERITAGE BOOKS, INC.

Books, CDs, and more—Worldwide

For our listing of thousands of titles see our website
at
www.HeritageBooks.com

Published 2007 by
HERITAGE BOOKS, INC.
Publishing Division
65 East Main Street
Westminster, Maryland 21157-5026

International Standard Book Number: 978-0-7884-2562-2

Dedicated to
Ernest and Eula Jackson
and
the American Indian

Contents

Chapter 1

Treaties and Depots of Death

Before the white man came and gained supremacy pushing onward over all the lands of the American frontier, there were many Indian communities that thrived on its bounty where they enjoyed the freedom and choice to experience life in accordance to their own faith and design. Forced by powers greater than their own, these tribes of peoples native to American soil were ruthlessly driven to reservations alien to them, to suffer the indignities and humiliations of an unwanted and submissive way of life - bringing poverty, disease, hunger, and death. A people removed from the warmth and hospitality of their simple fires, and swept forever from the generosity of the wild and untamed hunting grounds of their birth.

Several tribes were relocated to the Indian Nations, or Indian Territory, known today as the state of Oklahoma by the United States Government after treaties were signed. The largest part of the Indian Nations belonged to the "Five

1

Civilized Tribes," the Cherokees, Choctaws, Chickasaws, Creeks, and Seminoles.

The Treaty of New Echota, signed December 29, 1835, by the flickering of candlelight and the glow of a hearth's fire at New Echota, Georgia, ceded to the United States the whole Cherokee Nation territory east of the Mississippi River. This treaty, which was born at the old Cherokee capital about midnight in Elias Boudinot's crowded house, would eventually spawn a famous historical journey westward that would be appropriately called the Cherokee "Trail of Tears." A long and difficult road that would become littered with the graves of their loved ones, and the destruction of a people's soaring spirit.

The idea of being removed from their ancestral homelands was met with resistance by the greater body of the Cherokee people, to which General Wool, in command of troops to enforce the treaty, reported on February 18, 1837, that: "...it is, however, vain to talk to a people almost universally opposed to the treaty and who maintain that they never made such a treaty. So determined are they in their opposition that not one of all those who were present and voted at the council held but a day or two since, however poor or destitute, would receive either rations or clothing from the United States lest they might compromise themselves in regard to the treaty. These same people, as well as those in the mountains of North Carolina, during the summer past, preferred living upon the roots and sap of trees rather than receive provisions from the United States, and thousands, as I have been informed, had no other food for weeks. Many have said they will die before they will leave the country."[1]

While in the process of his duties of bringing the Cherokee into submission, General Wool, being moved to sympathy, wrote in a letter concerning the ordeal, saying: "The whole scene since I have been in this country has been nothing but a heart-rending one, and such a one as I would be glad to get rid of as soon as circumstances will permit. Because I am firm and decided, do not believe I would be unjust. If I could, and could not do them a greater kindness, I would remove every Indian to-morrow beyond the reach of the white men, who, like vultures, are watching, ready to pounce upon their prey and strip them of everything they have or expect from the government of the United States. Yes, sir, nineteen-twentieths, if not ninety-nine out of every hundred, will go penniless to the West."[2]

Further woes were expressed by Major Ridge, principle leader of the minority Ridge party to sign the treaty, in a letter to President Andrew Jackson, he addressed him about the "griefs and afflictions from the acts of the white people." He complains about the loss of the Cherokee lands and how the whites were "preparing to fleece" money accrued from the treaty. Major Ridge went on to say in the letter, that: "We found our plantations taken either in whole or in part by the Georgians - suits instituted against us for back rents for our farms. These suits are commenced in the inferior courts, with the evident design that, when we are ready to remove, to arrest our people, and on these vile claims to induce us to compromise for our own release, to travel with our families. Thus our funds will be fliched from our people, and we shall be compelled to leave our country as beggars and in want.

"Even the Georgia laws, which deny us our oaths, are thrown aside, and notwithstanding the cries of our people, and protestation of our innocence and peace, the lowest classes of the white people are flogging the Cherokees with cowhides, hickories, and clubs. We are not safe in our houses - our people are assailed by day and night by the rabble. Even justices of the peace and constables are concerned in this business. This barbarous treatment is not confined to men, but the women are stripped also and whipped without law or mercy...Send regular troops to protect us from these lawless assaults, and to protect our people as they depart for the West. If it is not done, we shall carry off nothing but the scars of the lash on our backs, and our oppressors will get all the money. We talk plainly, as chiefs having property and life in danger, and we appeal to you for protection...."[3]

Chief John Ross and the Ross party offered the greatest opposition to the Treaty of Echota, but the United States, in order to divide and conquer, accepted the treaty as binding on the entire Cherokee Nation.4 The treaty created a great division of animosity between the Ridge party and the Ross party; and in the future their tempers would flare.

Concerning the stiff opposition that came from the Ross party, one agent reported, that: "The whole Nation of eighteen thousand persons is with him, the few - about three hundred - who made the treaty having left the country - as Ridge, Boudinot, and others - who remained to assist in carrying it into execution. It is evident, therefore, that Ross and his party are in fact the Cherokee Nation...I believe that the mass of the Nation, particularly the mountain Indians, will stand or fall with Ross...."5

By May 26, 1838, the allotted time for the Cherokee to remove themselves to the west and Indian Territory, General Winfield Scott, along with sufficient troops, infantry, cavalry, and artillery, was assigned the task of forcing the remaining Cherokees, about 15,000, to their awaiting inevitable destiny.6 However, the few Cherokee who took to the sanctuary of the ancestral hills they knew so well and were never found, became known as the Eastern Cherokee.7

General Scott, in giving fair warning beforehand on May 10, declared in a proclamation that "troops already occupy many positions...and thousands and thousands are approaching from every quarter to render resistance and escape alike hopeless...Will you, then, by resistance compel us to resort to arms...or will you by flight seek to hide yourselves in mountains and forests and thus oblige us to hunt you down?"8

The troops were under orders from General Scott to construct stockade forts of split logs, to be sharpened and set upright into the ground for the purpose of housing captured Indians for removal. The camps were to be located at various places throughout the Cherokee countryside and manned by militia: in Tennessee, at the old agency, on Hiwassee

(Calhoun), and Ross' Landing (Chattanooga); and at Gunter's Landing (Guntersville), in Alabama.[9]

General Scott's soldiers were dispatched in squads with orders to hunt down and capture renegade Indians "with rifle and bayonet" and search out "every small cabin hidden away in the coves or by the sides of mountain streams, to seize and bring in as prisoners all the occupants, however or wherever they might be found."[10] The troops were relentless in their quest, and fulfilled their unpleasant duties as ordered. "Families at dinner were startled by the sudden gleam of bayonets in the doorway and rose up to be driven with blows and oaths along the weary miles of trail that led to the stockade."[11] No stone was left unturned, as Scott's men combed the precious Cherokee countryside; the white man's object of covet and affection. Houses were quickly surrounded by the soldiers, and their occupants confronted suddenly and without warning. "Men were seized in their fields or along the road, women were taken from their wheels and children from their play."[12] Ripped from their lives and all that they had known, with fear and indignation, some turned hopelessly "for one last look as they crossed the ridge, they saw their homes in flames, fired by the lawless rabble that followed on the heels of the soldiers...."[13]

The white outlaws, like hungry wolves, wasted no time to loot and pillage; reminiscent of the "Burnt District" caused by General Thomas Ewing's Military Order Number 11 of August 25, 1863, during the Civil War. The order forced the evacuation of about 20,000 Missourians from four western Missouri counties on a great mass exodus, which left their homes and everything they owned at the mercy of lawless Kansans who made quick work of their greedy opportunity.[14]

In a mad zest for gain, these lawless men of the white race desecrated "Indian graves, to rob them of the silver pendants and other valuables deposited with the dead."[15] One volunteer from Georgia, who later served as a colonel for the

Confederacy, made a comparison to the appalling treatment of the Indians, stating that: "I fought through the civil war and have seen men shot to pieces and slaughtered by thousands, but the Cherokee removal was the cruelest work I ever knew."[16]

Herded into the concentration camps, that had been prepared to detain these people, they became sick due to the food they were forced to eat. In James Mooney's *Myths of the Cherokee* he writes about the rations that the people received, saying that they "were of flour and other provisions to which they were unaccustomed and which they did not know how to prepare properly."[17] There were outbreaks of measles, whooping cough, and other diseases - hundreds died as they dropped like flies in these emigration depots of suffering and death.[18]

History will long remember and search for proper rhyme or reason to this sort of justice, when considering the Native Americans who were rounded up in their own homeland with rifle and bayonet and prodded into stockades to await death, or removal. Those that survived the camps would be forced to abandon the graves of their loved ones, the richness of the land and way of life that had served them and those before them, and everything familiar that they held dear. They would meander down a sorrowful path not knowing what might lie ahead of them in their future, or even if they would survive long enough to reach it. Many would no doubt wonder if their captors would spare them, and if they were to live what sort of land were they to be taken to - would it support them - would they be allowed to stay there or would it also be taken as well somewhere down the road? These questions must have ran through their troubled minds over and over again as they plodded along the road that stretched out before them. The elements relentless on their tired bodies and spirits as it made each day another challenge to overcome. Their condition daily deteriorated one step at a time. These Native American sojourners who were now broken in spirit and conquered, would walk for hundreds and hundreds of miles in fear and uncertainty over a "trail where they cried."

> Looking back, thinking of the sacredness of it all,
> The bounty and their ancestors call;
> Children, the old, and the graves,
> Lost forever to the white man's avarice crave.

Chapter 2

A Tearful Journey
to the Civil War

In the process of building a powerful nation a great many tribes of Indian Americans were crushed to annihilation, taken by any means necessary to live out their generations not as the eagle soars or the buffalo roam, but as helpless and hopeless victims doomed to the life of the reservation, or the confines of Oklahoma Indian Territory. The march west to the Nations would be costly to various tribes and hit the Cherokee where it hurt, and cause a throe of pain that would leave them forever searching for justice and their former glory.

As for the Cherokee removal from the east and from the various stockades there, it began in the heat of the summer which caused a great many to die. For this reason, Chief Ross and other leaders proposed to General Scott that they wait until the fall to continue the emigration, to which he agreed.

In October of 1838, some by way of the river, but most,

9

about 13,000 proceeded overland leaving the detention camps and their native homeland behind to the fate of the trail and the mercy of the Long Knives. Packed like animals into 645 wagons, "the sick, the old people, and the smaller children, with the blankets, cooking pots, and other belongings..." made their way westward with "the rest on foot or on horses."[1]

The sad and dejected Cherokee procession was marched like "an army, regiment after regiment, the wagons in the center, the officers along the line and the horsemen on the flanks and at the rear."[2] They slept in the crowded wagons and upon the ground with nothing to protect them from the elements. Each day the tribe lessoned in number "by the tens and twenties" along the "march of death," due to ill treatment and exposure of the "January blast." [3]

At Hopkinsville, Kentucky, "the noted chief White-path, in charge of a detachment, sickened and died. His people buried him by the roadside, with a box over the grave and poles with streamers around it, that the others coming on behind might note the spot and remember him."[4]

The freezing and driving sleet and snow of the cold winter weather was in contrast in comparison to the dreadful hot and arid dog days of summer they had just previously experienced in the concentration camps; but now, at the Mississippi River, at Cape Girardeau, Missouri, and at Green's Ferry, south of there, they suffered and perished from pneumonia, fatigue, and the lack of proper winter protection. Chief John Ross' wife Quate Martin Ross (also called Elizabeth Ross), who offered up her own blanket to a needy child who was sick, later died as a result of pneumonia in Little Rock, Arkansas, and was buried at a cemetery lot that was owned by Albert Pike who later became a Brigadier General for the Confederate States of America.[5] Other detachments traveled a more northern route by way of Springfield, Mo., "because those who had gone before [through northern Arkansas] had killed off all the game along the direct route."[6]

The inhuman trek which the multitude of Cherokee were made to march, took its toll on the most innocent - babies, children, and the old. Taking into account the number of silent graves that were left at the depots of death; along the trail of tears; and of those souls who died soon after their arrival to Indian Territory, is a staggering total of probably over 4,000 lost Cherokee. This surely must rank as one of the world's worst disasters and atrocities perpetrated on human life.

The tearful six month journey ended March 26, 1839, to the sound of a proud and resilient people rising up from their despair. However, the past would not cease to haunt them, as old wounds of the Treaty of New Echota would be reopened and once more spill Indian blood. The feud between the Ross party and the Ridge party came to a head, when: "Major Ridge was waylaid and shot close to the Arkansas line, his son [John Ridge] was taken from bed and cut to pieces with hatchets, while [Elias] Boudinot [a nephew of Major Ridge] was treacherously killed at his home at Park Hill, Indian Territory, all three being killed upon the same day, June 22, 1839."[7]

In a report to the Secretary of war dated June 24, 1839, agent Stokes offered the gory details, saying: "The murder of Boudinot was treacherous and cruel. He was assisting some workmen in building a new house. Three men called upon him and asked for medicine. He went off with them in the direction of Wooster's, the missionary, who keeps medicine, about three hundred yards from Boudinot's. When they got about half way two of the men seized Boudinot and the other stabbed him, after which the three cut him to pieces with their knives and tomahawks. This murder taking place within two miles of the residence of John Ross, his friends were apprehensive it might be charged to his connivance; and at this moment I am writing there are six hundred armed Cherokee around the dwelling of Ross, assembled for his protection. The murders of the two Ridge's and Boudinot are certainly of the late Cherokee emigrants, and, of course, adherents of Ross, but I can not yet believe that Ross has encouraged the outrage...."[8]

One fiery Cherokee of the Ridge party, a nephew of Major

Ridge and brother of Elias Boudinot, was Stand Watie (Degataga OO-Watee), who became the new Ridge party leader after the murders. Watie was born on December 12, 1806, in the old Cherokee nation, near present-day Rome, Georgia, to a Cherokee father and a half-Cherokee mother. After the murders of his brother, uncle, and cousin, Stand Watie vowed to get revenge, and as a result, there followed a number of killings between the Ross and the Ridge parties.[9]

As a signer and advocate of the Treaty of New Echota, Stand Watie arrived early on to Indian Territory in 1837 with his family. He located in an area reportedly first known as "Cross Hollers," which was renamed "Honey Creek Town" after it grew into a larger hub of activity. The town that exists in that area now is known as Southwest City, Missouri, located one mile north of the Mason-Dixon line on the edge of Oklahoma, where the state lines of Oklahoma, Arkansas and Missouri join together. County records show that many of the people who made their homes in the Honey Creek area were southerners, who brought slaves with them. During the Civil War, General Sterling Price would train his Confederate troops in an area called Cowskin Prairie about five miles north of Honey Creek Town. Many period artifacts have been recovered from there, relics of those men who would later fight in such bloody battles as Wilson's Creek, near Springfield, Missouri, (known as Oak Hills by the Confederates), and Pea Ridge, near Pea Ridge, Arkansas, (or by the South as Elk Horn Tavern).[10]

In 1843, Stand Watie would marry Sarah C. Bell and father three sons and two daughters. It was said that he was a man who spoke few words but put careful thought into his actions, a powerful ally and a formidable opponent. He worked very hard in the Honey Creek area as a businessman who owned farmland, mills, and a store in the area. Watie wasted no time to organize men to protect the Ridge party; this action left Chief Ross and his family no alternative but to flee to nearby Fort Gibson for refuge, where they were kept in safe keeping by the United States Army that was based there.[11]

Several skirmishes were fought in and around the Honey Creek area during the Civil War, between Union and Confederates. Residence also had to contend with bushwhackers and guerillas who haunted the region robbing, foraging crops, and stealing their livestock. Even the Indian Territory would not escape the ravages of the Civil War, with Union Kansas to the north, Confederate Arkansas to the east, Confederate Texas to the south, and the divided border state of Missouri to the northeast.

An old Indian trace also passed through Indian Territory which came to be used by the military as a supply-line, it was called the Texas Road, or the Fort Scott-Fort Gibson Military Road. The Nations would become a battleground during the War Between the States, and the five civilized tribes would be drawn into the chaos and destine to participate in the white man's war.

Choosing to side with the Southern cause, Stand Watie, was soon commissioned as a Colonel in the Confederacy. The tribes who once shed tears of great sorrow along the trail of death, removed from their eastern homeland by force would, not many years later fight and die not just in Indian Territory but in Arkansas and Missouri; and in 1862 at the 1st Battle of Newtonia (Missouri), Indians of the Blue would face Indians of the Gray in the din and roar of mortal combat.

In July of 1861 Colonel Stand Watie began to organize and recruit his Cherokee Mounted Rifles at an abandoned military post called Fort Wayne, in Indian Territory, just west of Maysville, Arkansas. Watie and his Cherokee Mounted Rifles would go on to fight in many Civil War battles; and on May 10, 1864, he would become the only Indian to attain the rank of Brigadier General for either the North or the South. Watie would also have the distinction of being the last Confederate general to surrender, including his Indian force, which he did to Lieutenant Colonel A.C. Matthews at Doaksville, Choctaw Nation (Oklahoma), on June 23, 1865; almost three months after General Robert E. Lee's surrender at Appomattox, Virginia.[12]

While on a visit to Honey Creek, General Stand Watie died suddenly on September 9, 1871. A Mason of high degree, he was buried with a Masonic ceremony at the Old Ridge-Polson Cemetery, Delaware County, Oklahoma, just west of Southwest City, Missouri. On May 25, 1921, the United Daughters of the Confederacy of Oklahoma unveiled an impressive marble stone quarried from the hills of his native Georgia homeland, in honor of his heroic service to the Southern cause.[13]

The Civil War caused a great division within the tribes of Indian Territory. With their southern roots and sympathies, and as slaveholders, many tribe members were compelled to side with the Confederacy; and possibly, past sour encounters with the Federal government may have also played a roll in their decision to sympathize with the South. The Ridge party, which was of course headed by Stand Watie, was backed by a secret secession organization called the Knights of the Golden Circle. However, the Ross party, headed by John Ross was backed by a pro-Union organization called the Kitoowah Society, that became known as the Pin Indians; named for pins they wore to symbolize their customs and traditions.[14]

On October 7, 1861, at Tahlequah, Indian Territory, with Confederate Commissioner General Albert Pike present, the Cherokee Nation joined the Confederacy along with the Creeks, Choctaws, Chickasaw, Seminole, Osage, Comanche, and others already committed to the cause.[15] In an annual report on the Cherokee Nation to the Bureau of Ethnology, concerning the effects of the Civil War and other problems to the Indian Nations, it read: "The events of the war brought to them more of desolation and ruin than perhaps to any other community. Raided and sacked alternately, not only by the Confederate and Union forces, but by the vindictive ferocity and hate of their own factional divisions, their country became a blackened and desolate waste. Driven from comfortable homes, exposed to want, misery, and the elements, they perished like sheep in a snow storm. Their houses, fences, and other improvements were burned, their orchards destroyed, their flocks and herds slaughtered or driven off, their schools broken up, their schoolhouses given to the flames, and their churches and public buildings subjected to a similar fate; and that entire portion of their country which had been occupied by their settlements was distinguishable from the virgin prairie only by the scorched and blackened chimneys and the plowed but now neglected fields."[16]

For scores of years Native Americans sought to retain their lot in life on the American frontier. They found and enjoyed the beauty that was in its streams, woodlands, and prairies; and in these places they freely hunted, planted, and multiplied. They provided for, and embraced the love of friends and family, through the strength and ingenuity by which they were endowed. To protect these things that were important to them, when necessary, they fought and killed red men and white men alike.

In an ever changing world its inhabitants has witnessed, throughout history, the rise and fall of many great civilizations and cultures. The earth's precious lands and resources has often times been an object of covet to those who would possess it, and its riches. In modern history, the expansion of a certain culture has verged into a nation of many races who now inhabit the vast, and now crowded Native American homelands of North America.

In the early days of the American frontier these so called "savages," who had managed well existing in such a beautiful and broad landscape for centuries, were suddenly forced by bayonet and at gunpoint to a future and region chosen for them with limited boundaries; their removal so vicious and cruel as to cause the death and suffering of thousands. Yet, when out of the ashes of these trails and tribulations they begin to build afresh, civil war rears its ugly head as the white man begins to wage a costly war - pitting brother against brother.

Once again, Indian lives are torn asunder and they are forced to make decisions that would hurl them into that bloody conflict. What they endured in the east being captured and herded into the suffering of the relocation camps, and the trail west where so many fell along the way, left them in new surroundings with additional troubles to face in the near future. The tribes of the Indian Nations would be swept up in the chaos and carnage to fight for the North and South in the American Civil War, which would leave their territory in ruins - a wasteland of more grief and destruction.

Chapter 3

Resistance is Futile

The white conquest in the East proved then, that to all Native Americans throughout the land, resistance is futile. The savagery which was perpetrated upon them to colonize and expand the United States of America left in its path many atrocities along the way, from its colonial beginnings to the final horrors of the massacre at Wounded Knee in 1890; only one of many historical tragedies of the American Indian Wars. It would mark for all times the end of their former prosperity and way of life.

Sounds of the Old West still reverberate tales of gloom and outrage when bringing to remembrance the hollow and empty promises made by the U.S. government, that the displaced Indians would be able to possess the West from that time on "while the grasses grow and the rivers flow." They would instead only dream and pine over what was and what might have been.

In 1861 at the outbreak of the Civil War, the Federal

government found itself occupied not only with the ongoing Indian affairs but also with the issue of slavery and states rights, as southern states were seceding one after the other. Once again, resisting the inevitable birth pangs of the white man's America, left the newly colonized Indian Territories and its struggling inhabitants no alternative but to chose between them.

In a letter dated January 29, 1861, to Principle Chief John Ross of the Cherokee Nation, the desire to win his loyalties for the Southern cause was expressed by Henry M. Rector the governor of Arkansas, which read: "Sir: It may now be regarded as almost certain that the States having slave property within their borders will, in consequence of repeated Northern aggressions, separate themselves and withdraw from the Federal Government.

"South Carolina, Alabama, Florida, Mississippi, Georgia, and Louisiana have already, by action of the people, assumed this attitude. Arkansas, Missouri, Tennessee, Kentucky, Virginia, North Carolina, and Maryland will probably pursue the same course by the 4th of March next. Your people, in their institutions, productions, latitude, and natural sympathies, are allied to the common brotherhood of the slaveholding States. Our people and yours are natural allies in war and friends in peace. Your country is salubrious and fertile, and possesses the highest capacity for future progress and development by the application of slave labor. Besides this, the contiguity of our territory with yours induces relations of so intimate a character as to prelude the idea of discordant or separate action.

"It is well established that the Indian country west of Arkansas is looked to by the incoming administration of Mr. Lincoln as fruitful fields, ripe for the harvest of abolitionism, freesoilers, and Northern mountebanks.

"We hope to find in your people friends willing to co-operate with the South in defense of her institutions, her honor, and her firesides, and with whom the slaveholding States are willing to share a common future, and to afford protection commensurate with your exposed condition and your subsisting monetary interests with the General Government.

"As a direct means of expressing to you these sentiments, I have dispatched my aide-de-camp, Lieut. Col. J.J. Gaines, to confer with you confidentially upon these subjects, and to report to me any expressions of kindness and confidence that you may see proper to communicate to the governor of Arkansas, who is your friend and the friend of your people."[1]

Wanting to remain neutral, John Ross, attempted to respectfully and peacefully resist involvement in the white man's war. One such letter he received from Confederate Commander Brigadier General Ben McCulloch dated June 12, 1861, reveals the pressure the Cherokee leader was under to commit his people to the bloody conflict. "Sir: Having been sent by my Government (the Confederate States of America) to take command of the district embracing the Indian Territory, and to guard it from invasion by the people of the North, I take the first opportunity of assuring you of the friendship of my Government, and desire that the Cherokees and other tribes in the Territory unite their fortunes with the Confederacy. I hope that you, as chief of the Cherokees, will meet me with the same feelings of friendship that actuate me in coming among you, and that I may have your hearty co-operation in one common cause against a people who are endeavoring to deprive us of our rights. It is not my desire to give offense, or interfere with any of your rights or wishes, and shall not do so unless circumstances compel me. The neutral position you wish to maintain will not be molested without good cause. In the meantime those of your people who are in favor of joining the Confederacy must be allowed to organize into military companies as Home Guards, for the purpose of defending themselves in case of invasion from the North. This of course will be in accordance with the views you expressed to me, that in case of an invasion from the North you would lead your men yourself to repel it. Should a body of men march into your Territory from the North, or if I have an intimation that a body is in line of march for the Territory from that quarter, I must assure you that I will at once advance into your country, if I deem it advisable...."[2]

In reply to General McCulloch's letter, Chief Ross, in an attempt to clarify and set the record straight with the hopes of continuing to keep his neutral position, wrote on June 17, 1861, that concerning "the pending conflict between the United States and Confederate States, I have already signified my purpose to take no part in it whatever, and have admonished the Cherokee people to pursue the same course. The determination to adopt that course was the result of considerations of law and policy, and seeing no reason to doubt its propriety, I shall adhere to it in good faith, and hope that the Cherokee people will not fail to follow my example. I have not been able to see any reason why the Cherokee Nation should take any other course, for it seems to me to be dictated by their treaties and sanctioned by wisdom and humanity. It ought not to give ground for complaint to either side, and should cause our rights to be respected by both. Our country and institutions are our own. However small the one and humble the others, they are as sacred and valuable to us as are those of your own populous and wealthy State to yourself and people. We have done nothing to bring about the conflict in which you are engaged with your own people, and I am unwilling that my people shall become its victims, and I am determined to do no act that shall furnish any pretext to either of the contending parties to overrun our country and destroy our rights....

"Your demand that those people of the nation who are in favor of joining the Confederacy be allowed to organize into military companies as Home Guards, for the purpose of defending themselves in case of invasion from the North, is most respectfully declined. I cannot give my consent to any such organization for very obvious reasons: First, it would be a palpable violation of my position as a neutral; second, it would place in our midst organized companies not authorized by our laws but in violation of treaty, and who would soon become efficient instruments in stirring up domestic strife and creating internal difficulties among the Cherokee people. As in this connection you have misapprehended a remark made in conversation at our interview some eight or ten days ago, I hope you will allow me to repeat what I did say. I informed you that I had taken a neutral position, and would maintain it honestly, but that in case of a foreign invasion, old as I am, I would assist in repelling it. I have not signified any purpose as to an invasion of our soil and an interference with our rights from the United States or Confederate States, because I have apprehended none, and cannot give my consent to any...."[3]

On August 21, 1861, the Cherokee people gathered together at Tahlequah to make decisions and express their concerns. The meeting was called by the executive of the Cherokee Nation, and about 4,000 turned out to participate. At the meeting, Chief John Ross addressed the crowd in attendance and spoke of the hostility between the United States and the Confederate States of America. He warned that siding with one or the other could cause serious problems with their friends and neighbors, so he advised them to remain neutral. Ross said that: "In time of peace, enjoy peace together; in time of war, if war must come, fight together. As brothers live, as brothers die. While ready and willing to defend our firesides from the robber and murderer, let us not make war wantonly against the authority of the United or Confederate States, but avoid conflict with either, and remain strictly on our own soil...."[4]

However, only a few days before this peaceful gathering at Tahlequah, on August 10, 1861, a small Indian force under Captain Joel Mayes (who was part Cherokee),[5] had already taken part to some degree on the battleground of the ghastly engagement at Wilson's Creek; which was fought a few miles southwest of Springfield, Missouri. According to Colonel Thomas L. Snead of Confederate General Sterling Price's staff concerning the battle, he said: "Never before - considering the number engaged - had so bloody a battle been fought upon

American soil; seldom has a bloodier one been fought on any modern field."[6]

But about Native Americans being allowed to take part in the war, Colonel Snead had this to say: "Missouri, with her 100,000 men and resources greater than those of all the cotton States together, was worth nothing to the Confederacy in comparison with two or three regiments of semi-civilized Indians who ought never to have been allowed to cross the borders of their own territory."[7]

John Ross' commitment to remain neutral, although some Indians in the territory were slaveholders, would not exempt them from the chaos and pressures applied by abolitionists, secessionists, and civil war. Many siding early on with the Confederates after their decisive victory at Wilson's Creek, but as the madness of the war continued, so did the confusion of loyalty. They would have little choice to resist the call to arms as the Indian Nations would go to battle with themselves, the Confederates, and the United States. Regardless of their boundaries they would fight, not only in many locations in Oklahoma Indian Territory, but in Missouri and Arkansas.

Chapter 4

Early Southern Victories

The old Indian ways had now only become haunting memories of the way they were. Far removed from those more chosen times, they might dare inwardly to dream within their hearts and minds of what it was like before the grave-littered tear-covered trail westward they were forced to tread.

Now, in the near distance, the death dealing thunder of big guns and the hissing and screaming of musket lead echoed in the east. A war was waging on between the States - at Ft. Sumter in South Carolina, at Carthage in Missouri, and at Manassas in Virginia. These were early Southern victories that would encourage many Native Americans of the Indian Nations to side with the Confederacy. A tide-changing major battle in southwestern Missouri would prompt many more to falsely think that the South could win the war; but none conceived that it was only the beginning of the long years that would cause the death of thousands, and only instead spill in vain the costly blood of failure.

By mid-July 1861 Union General Nathaniel Lyon was drilling about 6,200 troops at Springfield, Missouri, building up supplies and begging for reinforcements; about 500 of these soldiers were poorly equipped and undisciplined "Home Guards."[1] When General Lyon entered the town of Springfield, it was recalled that: "The chroniclers of the city still delight to tell of the brave appearance that he made that day, as he dashed through the streets on his iron-gray horse, under escort of a body-guard of ten stalwart troopers enlisted from among the German butchers of St. Louis for that especial duty and how the fearless horsemanship and defiant bearing of these bearded warriors, mounted on powerful chargers and armed to the teeth with great revolvers and massive swords, their heroic size and ferocious aspect gave luster to the entry into the chief city of the Southwest...."[2]

Lyon's continued appeals to General John C. Fremont in St. Louis for additional troops fell on deaf ears, and on August 1-2, 1861, Lyon moved 23 miles south of Springfield with his infantry, cavalry, and eighteen artillery pieces, and engaged Confederate General Sterling Price's advance guard at a place called Dug Springs. However, after a several hour skirmish Lyon believed that he was getting to far from his supplies, and Springfield, so he fell back reaching it on the 5th. "During those blistering August days the men marched with bleeding feet and parched lips, Lyon himself urging forward the weary and footsore stragglers."[3]

By August 6, after the fighting at Dug Springs, Price's total force of about 12,000 were encamped in the area of Wilson's Creek; which is about 10 miles southwest of Springfield. On the 9th Lyon received word that reinforcements would not be sent and he would have to do the best that he could. In a brave and loyal reply Lyon wrote his final letter to Fremont, saying: "General - I have just received your note of the 6th inst., by special messenger. I retired to this place, as I have before informed you, reaching here on the 5th. The enemy followed to within ten miles of here. He has taken a strong position, and is recruiting his supplies of horses, mules, and provisions by forages into the surrounding country. His large force of mounted men enables him to do this without much annoyance from me. I find my position extremely embarrassing, and am at present unable to determine whether I shall be able to maintain my ground or forced to retire. I shall hold my ground as long as possible, though I may, without knowing how far, endanger the safety of my entire force with its valuable material, being induced, by the important considerations involved, to take this step. The enemy yesterday made a show of force about five miles distant, and has doubtless a full purpose of making an attack on me. Very respectfully, your obedient servant, N. Lyon."[4]

On the night of the 9th Lyon's Federals left Springfield in an attempt to surprise the enemy at Wilson's Creek, before Price and McCulloch could organize an attack on him.[5] About 1,000 were left behind to guard the supply base at Springfield.

The battle began at daybreak August 10, 1861, with Union forces numbering about 5,400 strong. However, Union Colonel Franz Sigel was sent to the south with about 1,200 with the hopes of flanking the Confederates. This left Lyon with only about 4,200 men to spring his surprise attack. The Southern forces were taken off guard initially, and over 4,500 of them "were stampeded and lost in the woods."[6]

For about half an hour the Federals fought fiercely to overrun a hill which came to be known as "Bloody Hill," and after doing so, the Confederates fell back and reformed and for over 5 hours the bloody contest for it raged. "The carnage became frightful. The slopes of Bloody Hill were strewn with ghastly corpses...Price charged time and again up the slope, only to be repulsed by the Federals lying on the crest."[7]

Colonel Thomas L. Snead, in his article *The First Year of the War in Missouri*, described the Battle of Wilson's Creek as one of "the stubbornest and bloodiest battles of the war" as "Lyon's main attack was met by Price with about 3200 Missourians, and Churchill's regiment and Woodruff's battery, both from Arkansas. His left was met and driven back by McIntosh with a part of McCulloch's brigade (the Third Louisiana and McIntosh's regiment). McCulloch then took some companies of the Third Louisiana and parts of other commands, and with them attacked and routed Sigel (who had been sent to attack the rear), capturing five of his guns. This done, Pearce's Arkansas brigade, which up to this time had not fired a gun, was sent to reinforce Price. Lyon, seeing that the supreme moment had come, and that the day would be surely lost if he did not overwhelm Price before the Arkansas could reinforce him, now brought forward every available man, and was putting them into the fight, when his horse [the iron gray] was killed, and himself wounded in the head...."[8]

Lyon, the brave Union leader, now wounded in the head and reportedly in the leg as well, was now "begrimed and bloody," Riding again to the front on a new horse he had gotten from Major Samuel Sturgis, "swinging his hat and calling to his men to follow,"[9] he quickly ordered General Sweeney to lead the 1st Iowa forward for "one more charge."[10] Suddenly, as he was at the head of the column he was shot through the left side of his breast, and at last, said to his orderly, Private Ed Lehman, "Lehman, I'm going," then he "passed his spirit through the battle-clouds to realms where is everlasting peace."[11] The place on the battlefield where Lyon fell became known as the "Bloody Point." A granite marker dedicated in 1928 marks the historic spot at the Wilson's Creek National Battlefield.

After the death of Lyon, Major Sturgis assumed command of the Union forces but, after about half an hour with the ammunition almost exhausted, the order was given to fall back to Springfield. The bloodbath was over. Left on the battleground were those with mangled limbs; "with bowels torn out, with faces shattered, heads torn to pieces, handsome countenances distorted into ghastly, grinning objects - dead men everywhere.

"Wounded men everywhere. Crawling about, delirious

with pain and agony; lying prone and almost motionless, starring up into the blue sky, dying slowly and making no sign; shrieking, groaning, cursing, praying, imploring help, begging for a bandage, for water, lying quietly, laughing even, - wounded men everywhere. In hospitals, under trees, in tents, in houses, in stables, with surgeons probing and cutting and carving and sawing and clumsily bandaging...."[12]

One of the houses which served as a hospital after the battle, which is on the east side of the battlefield, is the "Ray House." Built about 1852, the John A. Ray House was located on the Old Wire Road and also served as a post office and a flag stop for the Butterfield Overland Stage. It is part of the Wilson's Creek National Battlefield.

The loss of human life as a result of the Battle of Wilson's Creek (or Oak Hills by the Confederates), numbered over 1,300 for the Union, and more than 1,200 for the Confederates. The dead were buried by the Confederates, and it was said that fourteen Union soldiers were thrown in an old well near the battlefield and thirty-four were put into a "sinkhole," but were later reburied with honor in Springfield. It was also reported that portions of bodies were seen "several days after the battle, strewn along near the road, having been torn by dogs and hogs and buzzards. Skulls, bones, etc., indicating that at least a dozen corpses had been left above ground...."[13]

Although Native Americans did not play a major role in this bloody drama, it did create momentum for the Confederate cause and its number of recruits mustered from the Indian Nations. Unfortunately, the time had also come for the war to afflict them in their own backyards, bringing even more death and destruction to the West.

Chapter 5

Opothleyoholo's Stand

Faced with an American civil conflict in Indian Territory, thousands were being trained and organized for the game of war. Very soon the preferable sounds of peace and silence would be transformed, by struggle, and the deafening din of that deadly contest.

Confederate Colonel Douglas H. Cooper, a former U.S. Indian Agent, was in command of a regiment of the 1st Choctaw and Chickasaw Mounted Rifles. Brigadier General Albert Pike was in command over all of the Department of Indian Territory; a total of three regiments of Choctaw, Chickasaw, Cherokee, Creek, and Seminole Indians, organized for Confederate service. Also making preparations was Creek Chief Opothleyoholo (also known as Hopoeithleyohola or Opothle Yahola), who was gathering together a pro-Union force of "Loyal Creeks" and various other allies north of the Cimarron River in the Creek Nation. Colonel Cooper made several unsuccessful attempts to meet with the old Creek

Chief to come to a peaceful agreement, but, Opothleyoholo remained steadfast and loyal to the United States.[1]

Opothleyoholo was put to the test on November 19, 1861, in the first Civil War battle waged in the Indian Nations, as Cooper's Indian force and a regiment of Texas cavalry faced off with the stubborn loyal Creek Chief and his Union followers at a place called Round Mountain; Opothleyoholo was en route to Walnut Creek, Kansas, where a fort was being built. Seeing camp smoke and enemy scouts they thought they had located the possible camp of Opothleyoholo at Red Fork on the Arkansas River, so Cooper sent Lieutenant Colonel Quayle's Texans to investigate. However, finding that it was only a small abandoned campsite, Quayle pressed on about 4 miles more following enemy scouts with the hopes of finding Opothleyoholo's main camp. Suddenly, the Texans came under a deadly cyclone of whizzing lead from a large force appearing from the timber just ahead of them, which sent them in a hasty retreat - they had found Opothleyoholo. By the time Cooper and his Mounted Rifles arrived to reinforce Quayle it was nightfall, but their combined efforts soon forced Opothleyoholo to retire to the safety of the Northeast under the cover of darkness.

Colonel Cooper reported that: "Soon after daylight on the 20th the main camp of the enemy was entered, and it was found that they had precipitately abandoned it, leaving behind the chief's buggy, 12 wagons, flour, sugar, coffee, salt, & c., besides many cattle and ponies. Hopoeithleyohola's force in this engagement has been variously estimated at from 800 to 1,200 Creeks and Seminoles and 200 to 300 Negroes."[2]

The Battle of Round Mountain (or Red Forks), fought near present-day Yale, Oklahoma, became not only the first Civil War battle in Indian Territory but also the first stand taken by Opothleyoholo to resist Confederate authority. Cooper's losses were small, but about enemy losses he reported that, the "prisoners taken since the battle concur in stating the loss of the enemy [Opothleyoholo's] to have been about 110 killed and wounded."[3]

From this small but bloody beginning, the Civil War now had its Ft. Sumter in Indian Territory. Native Americans would go on to learn its awful lessons, learning amidst the roar and thunder of the white man's cannons and volleys of shrieking projectiles on many smoke filled battlegrounds.

Cooper and his Confederates, while camping at Tulsey Town (Tulsa), received word from an escaped prisoner of Opothleyoholo that 2,000 were preparing an attack. The place Opothleyoholo had chosen was a very strong position situated at a bend on Bird Creek, which was just north of Tulsey Town. The Creeks called it Fonta-hulwache, or Little High Shoals; but it was also known as Chusto-Talasah, or Caving Banks.

Colonel Cooper describes Opothleyoholo's position on the creek bank, in this way: "The creek made up to the prairie on the side of our approach in an abrupt, precipitous bank, some 30 feet in height, at places cut into steps, reaching near the top and forming a complete parapet, while the creek, being deep, was fordable but at certain points known only to the enemy. The opposite side, which was occupied by the hostile forces, was densely covered with heavy timber, matted undergrowth, and thickets, and fortified additionally by prostrate logs. Near the center of the enemy's line was a dwelling-house, a small corn-crib, and rail fence, situated in a recess of the prairie, at the gorge of a bend of the creek, of horseshoe form, about 400 or 500 yards in length. This bend was thickly wooded, and covered in front, near the house, with large interwoven weeds and grass, extending to a bench, behind which the enemy could lie and pour upon the advancing line his deadly fire in comparative safety, while the creek banks on either side covered the house by flank and reverse."[4]

The Confederate Creeks, under Colonel D.N. McIntosh, charged the Union Indians on the left in hand-to-hand combat driving them out of the woods and scattering them in all directions. The Choctaws and Chickasaws went to the right and rode into a steady stream of gunfire from the Union near a ravine on the creek. After dismounting they pushed

Opothleyoholo's Indians back, "contesting the ground with much obstinacy."5 With help from Lieutenant Colonel Quayle's Texas cavalry, Colonel Sim's Texans, and a charge by Captain Young's Choctaw and Chickasaw regiment, the Union Indians "were driven from their stronghold and pursued far into the bend, where, receiving on the flank an unexpected fire," according to Cooper's report, "the squadron took position at the house. Being then re-enforced by some men from Captains Reynolds', McCurtain's and Hall's companies, of the Choctaw and Chickasaw regiment, the conflict with the persistent foe was renewed with increased vigor, and after a fierce struggle the enemy was forced, with heavy loss, through the bend and across the creek."6

However, about 500 Union Indians forced some Confederates to retreat to the house where the fighting raged on at close quarters for about half an hour more - Opothleyoholo's men "alternately yielding and advancing and pouring upon [the Confederates] a galling fire."7 With the Confederate horses at risk in the rear, they became alarmed at losing them so they went to secure them, and then, reformed their line at a distance from the house. With night quickly approaching, so did the end of the fighting.

Once again, Opothleyoholo had made a brave stand at the Battle of Bird Creek against the Confederate secessionists to force him into submission. His woes were not yet over, in a few days the Southerners would catch up with him and his loyal band of Indians again, in the bitter cold and unforgivable winter weather where he would pay a high price for his Union loyalties.

On December 20, 1861, Confederate Colonel James McIntosh, responding to a call of additional troops by Colonel Cooper, arrived at Fort Gibson in Indian Territory to help deal with Opothleyoholo's resistance there. It was decided that McIntosh and his force of about 1,380 men would "march up the Verdigris River opposite the position held by the enemy, and then move directly upon him."8 While Cooper, strengthened by Major Whitfield's battalion, would "move up the Arkansas River and endeavor to get in the rear of Hopoeithleyohola's position on one of the tributaries of the Verdigris River, near the Big Bend of the Arkansas...On account of the scarcity of forage it was mutually determined that either force should attack the enemy on sight."9

About noon on December 26, 1861, McIntosh reached Shoal Creek, in an area known as Patriot Hills or Chustenahlah. Without warning, as Captain Short was crossing the stream, they were confronted from a high rugged timbered hill by "a heavy and continuous firing." McIntosh ordered Lieutenant Colonel Griffith's Texas cavalry to the right, and Colonel Young's Texans to the left. Moving up the center McIntosh sent Lieutenant Colonel Lane's South Kansas-Texas Regiment, Captain Bennett's Texans, and the Second Regiment of Arkansas Mounted Riflemen. The place that Opothleyoholo had chosen, left him a very good line of sight in which to observe the attack. Behind the natural safety of the trees and rocks were loyal Seminoles, under command of Chief Halek Tustenuggee;10 the rest lined the hilltop or beyond. The Union force totaled about 1,700 men.

In a report made by Confederate Colonel McIntosh dated January 1, 1862, about the Battle of Patriot Hills, he wrote: "...Between the rough and rugged side of the hill a space of 200 or 300 yards intervened of open ground. Each tree on the hill-side screened a stalwart warrior. It seemed a desperate undertaking to charge a position which appeared almost inaccessible, but the order to charge to the top of the hill met a responsive feeling from each gallant heart in the line, and at 12m.the charge was sounded, one wild yell from a thousand throats burst upon the air, and the living mass hurled itself upon the foe. The sharp report of the rifle came from every tree and rock, but on our brave men rushed, nor stopped until the summit of the hill was gained and we were mingled with the enemy...."11

Being pressed on the left the Union Indians moved toward the right, then, abandoning the hill and its natural places of safety they made their final stand at Opothleyoholo's main encampment site. After four hours of fierce battle, with his men and property scattered and broken up, the old Creek Chief was beaten and once again hastened toward Walnut Creek, Kansas. Arriving late, and taking up the chase for Opothleyoholo, was Colonel Stand Watie and about 300 of his Cherokees where they engaged the retreating rear guard of the Loyal Indians.

Colonel McIntosh reported that as a result of the Battle of Patriot Hills, his losses were 8 killed and 32 wounded; while he reported that Opothleyoholo lost about 250 in the fight. There were 160 women and children captured, 20 African Americans, "30 wagons, 70 yoke of oxen, about 500 Indian horses, several hundred head of cattle, 100 sheep," and a large quantity of other valuable property.[12]

Opothleyoholo's exodus into southern Kansas, was not unlike the tearful trail westward by the Cherokee during their removal after the Treaty of Echota. The cold freezing weather of late December and January took a heavy toll, especially upon the women and children, where some froze to death. Their suffering along the trail, and in the refugee camps in Kansas a few miles north of Indian Territory on the Verdigris River, left a sad and appalling untold tale of death and woe; while there, as many as 7,600 various tribes and other people sought sanctuary waiting for the mercy of spring to come and rescue them. However, by the time their savior would arrive, many poor victims of the frigid season would also lose their hands and feet to amputation.[13]

The price of the Civil War was rapidly draining the lifeblood from the people of the Indian Nations, while Opothleyoholo would cease to participate in the war, the bloodletting in Indian Territory would continue. The early success of the Confederacy would see other opportunities in the near future, one of which would task them very soon at a place called the Elkhorn Tavern, in extreme northern Arkansas on the Missouri border. A battle that would do much to help decide the fate of Missouri, and also a battle that would help to make a decision as to whether or not Native

Americans should fight outside the boundaries of Indian Territory.

Chapter 6

Tomahawkers and Scalpers

The beautiful scenic Ozark area in northern Arkansas, known as Pea "Vine" Ridge, was once caught in the deadly crossfire of the Civil War, in which Brigadier General Albert Pike's Confederate Indian troops participated in the fighting. Ironically, the Trail of Tears also passed through the battlefield where thousands of poor suffering Indian souls were marched on their way west - not many years before. Ironic too, were their deeds and terrifying war whoops given in retribution that echoed across the field of battle that day.

On the ridge overlooking the vast surroundings of "Sugar Creek Hollow," is the Elkhorn Tavern, that was situated on the Old Telegraph Road and had served as a stopping place for the Butterfield Overland Mail and stagecoach route to California until 1861. The tavern became a hospital during the battle where its owners, hiding in the basement, had to endure the oozing blood that dripped down upon them through the cracks in the Inn's floorboards. While visiting the Elkhorn Tavern after the war in 1887, Franz Sigel, who was a Brigadier General for the Union in the battle that was fought there, spoke about the owner and the tavern, saying: "Mr. Cox, who lived there in 1862, was obliged, with his mother and his young wife, to seek protection in the cellar, where they remained for two days, being under fire thirteen hours. Late in the war the tavern was burned, but Mr. Cox rebuilt it after the plan of the old one...."[1]

The Elkhorn Tavern vicinity was described in the Official Records by Union Major-General Samuel R. Curtis, in this way: "The valley of the creek is low, and from a quarter to a half mile wide. The hills are high on both sides, and the main road from Fayetteville [Arkansas] by Cross Hollow to Keetsville [Washburn, Missouri] intercepts the valley nearly at right angles. The road from Fayetteville by Bentonville [Arkansas] to Keetsville is quite a detour, but it also comes up the Sugar Creek Valley; a branch, however, takes off and runs nearly parallel to the main or Telegraph Road, some 3 miles from it. The Sugar Creek Valley, therefore, intercepts all these roads."[2]

Being moved to the west to take supreme command of the Confederate army was Major General Earl Van Dorn, and in the Boston Mountains of Arkansas the forces of Major General Sterling Price and Brigadier General Ben McCulloch were being combined; also joining up with the massive force was Brigadier General Albert Pike and his Indian troops. On March 4, 1862, Van Dorn began to move his newly formed army of about 16,000 north toward Pea Ridge, where Union Brigadier General Samuel R. Curtis and his force of about 10,500 were digging in along the frozen bluffs of Sugar Creek near the Elkhorn Tavern, a Union supply depot. Curtis had posted his army in a position to stop the Confederate advance into Missouri. Van Dorn's plan was to invade Missouri, capture St. Louis, and then cross the Mississippi River and take the war into the state of Illinois.[3]

When word arrived to General Curtis from his trusted scout, Wild Bill Hickok, that the Confederates were advancing upon their position, Curtis quickly tried to get a message to Union Brigadier General Franz Sigel to bring up his artillery; Sigel was at Bentonville eating breakfast at the Eagle Hotel. It was March 6 as a detachment of Sigel's clashed outside of Bentonville with Price's advance guard, which spoiled Sigel's breakfast and served as a prelude to a three day bloody ordeal, there, and on the 7th and 8th at nearby Leetown and Pea Ridge.4

About the battle that occurred near Bentonville that day, Sigel reported that: "From the moment we left the town, at 10:30 in the morning, until 3:30 o'clock in the afternoon, when we met the first re-enforcements - the Second Missouri, the Twenty-fifth Illinois, and a few companies of the Forty-fourth Illinois - we sustained three regular attacks, and were uninterruptedly in sight and under fire of the enemy....

"It would take too much time to go into the detail of this most extraordinary and critical affair, but as a matter of justice I feel it my duty to declare that according to my humble opinion never troops have shown themselves worthier to defend a great cause than on this day of the 6th of March."5

Van Dorn's hope of crushing Sigel at Bentonville almost came to pass, but Sigel was able to escape and join up with Curtis who by this time was faced off with Van Dorn near Pea Ridge - just out of reach of his big guns. Under the cloaking cover of darkness Van Dorn and Price attempted to move to the rear of Curtis in order to block the Federals from being able to retreat into Missouri on the Telegraph Road. McCulloch, Pike, and Stand Watie's Indians were in front of the Union army that was entrenched on the bluffs of Sugar Creek; the Confederates were moving to converge on Curtis at Pea Ridge and the Elkhorn Tavern. It was now the cold morning of March 7, 1862.

At Leetown the pony-mounted Indians did well when using the Ozark timber as an advantage but, as Pike reported, the Indians "would not face shells in the open ground."[6] Pike was scorned for his decision to let his Indians fight in a manner that was most familiar to them - with bow, arrow, and tomahawk.[7] With the help of Brigadier General James McIntosh's Texans, and Stand Watie's force, they were able to capture an artillery battery, or as the Indians called them "shooting wagons." In their jubilant celebration that followed, it was reported that the Cherokee warriors danced about their newly acquired field pieces adorning horse collars and rattling harness chains. The discovery of mangled, mutilated, and scalped Federals were later discovered on this portion of the battleground, due to the joyful overkill of Indian tomahawkers and scalpers. Their victory dance was short-lived, however, by Union shelling, which sent the Indians retreating to the cover of their precious trees.[8]

In one report made to Van Dorn, dated March 9, 1862, by order of Brigadier General S.R. Curtis, it read: "The general regrets that we find on the battle-field, contrary to civilized warfare, many of the Federal dead who were tomahawked, scalped, and their bodies shamefully mangled, and expresses a hope that this important struggle may not degenerate to a savage warfare."[9]

The dialog continued for some time over the appalling human atrocities that Pike's Indians left on the Pea Ridge battlefield, and on March 13, 1862, Curtis complains again, saying: "They shot arrows as well as rifles, and tomahawked and scalped prisoners."[10]

And further, concerning the same matter, Assistant Adjutant-General Dabney H. Maury, writing on March 14, 1862, to Union General Curtis, added this: "General: I am instructed by Major-General Van Dorn, commanding this district, to express to you his thanks and gratification on account of the courtesy extended by yourself and the officers under your command to the burial party sent by him to your camp on the 9th instant.

"He hopes you have been misinformed with regard to this matter, the Indians who formed part of his forces having for many years been regarded as civilized people. He will, however, most cordially unite with you in repressing the horrors of this unnatural war, and that you may co-operate with him to this end more effectually he desires me to inform you that many of our men who surrendered themselves prisoners of war were reported to him as having been murdered in cold blood by their captors, who were alleged to be Germans.

"The general commanding feels sure that you will do your part, as he will, in preventing such atrocities in future, and that the perpetrators of them will be brought to justice, whether German or Choctaw.

"The privileges which you extend to our medical officers will be reciprocated, and as soon as possible means will be taken for an exchange of prisoners."[11]

As the battle raged on Price's army was pressing Curtis on the east side, while McCulloch's southern veterans and Pike's two Indian regiments were engaged and marching to the west of Pea Ridge and Round Top under heavy fire. Then, in the afternoon as Confederate General Ben McCulloch rode out to make an assessment of the operations, the old soldier who fought Indians with Davy Crockett, Mexicans at the Battle of San Jacinto,[12] and commanded thousands of undaunted soldiers, was shot dead. Confederate hearts sank low when the tragic news spread among the troops like a town crier, that: "McCulloch is dead, McIntosh is dead, Herbert is dead!"[13]

When recalling the death of McCulloch and other Confederate leaders, Curtis wrote in his report on April 1, 1862, about the effect he believed it had on the outcome of the battle, saying: "The fall of General McCulloch, McIntosh, and other officers of the enemy, who fell early in the day, aided us in our final success at this most critical point; and the steady courage of officers and men in our lines chilled and broke down the hordes of Indians, cavalry, and infantry that were arrayed against us...."[14]

Concerning McCulloch and the others who perished at Pea Ridge, Earl Van Dorn, wrote on March 27, 1862, that: "No successes can repair the loss of the gallant dead who fell on this well-fought field. McCulloch was the first to fall. I had found him, in frequent conferences I had with him, a sagacious, prudent counselor, and a bolder soldier never died for his country."[15]

McCulloch's downcast Confederates continued their military efforts for awhile, but for lack of leadership the Federals began to scatter the enemy from the field. However, Price fared better with his eastern assault as his Missourians were able to eventually push the Federals back, and by nightfall with McCulloch's brokenhearted men joining up, the Confederates held Telegraph Road, Huntsville Road, and the Elkhorn Tavern. The first bloody day of fighting at Pea Ridge was over.

According to Union General Sigel: "The death of McCulloch was not only fatal to his troops, but also a most serious blow to Van Dorn. Until 2 o'clock on the 7th, the latter had confidently expected to hear of successful action against our left wing; but he received no answer to the dispatch he had sent, and began to push forward his own wing. He succeeded, and when night fell made his headquarters at Elkhorn Tavern, where Carr and Major Weston of our army had been in the morning...."[16]

When the morning of March 8, 1862, dawned on this breathtaking innocent countryside, the roll call of drums signaled Curtis' intent - he would attack the Confederates at Elkhorn. With the determined flag of the Union held high into the air, in clouds of blue-gray smoke and the thunderous reports of dueling cannon fire and hateful volleys of musketry, the brave Federals rushed on climbing over their own fallen comrades as they charged pell-mell against the deadly hope of victory.

Finally, with their ammunition running low, the Confederates were forced to withdraw from the ground they had held until mid-morning. Sigel reported that: "The rattling of musketry, the volleys, the hurrahs, did prove very soon that our troops were well at work in the woods, and that they were gaining ground rapidly...."[17]

And so Van Dorn's army hastened from the field, some of them traveled east on the Huntsville Road but the majority of them marched north on the Telegraph Road; Colonel Stand Watie's Indian warriors, who had remained faithful till the end, covered their retreat with a successful constant and heavy gunfire. The Battle of Pea Ridge (or Elkhorn Tavern), left about 1,000 men killed or wounded on each side.

In a few months Indians would again participate in the conflict, but this time in Missouri at a crucial area important to Union and Confederate alike. Indians of the North and South would clash mortally and fight against each other, once again causing controversy which would effect their future in the Civil War.

Chapter 7

Lead and Land

A few miles east of Neosho, Missouri, in an area known as Oliver's Prairie, is the small village of Newtonia where on September 30, 1862, the 1st Battle of Newtonia was fought. The engagement had the historical distinction of being the first major battle that involved Native Americans fighting against each other in the Civil War. A second significant battle also took place here on October 28, 1864, which had the distinction of being the last Civil War battle fought in Missouri involving regular army troops; it marked the end of Price's final invasion of his state.

The surrounding area was of importance to both the North and the South on account of the fertile prairie farmland, the availability of water, sturdy buildings, and the nearby mining town of Granby where the Confederates mined the lead that was used in the Battle of Wilson's Creek. After their loss at Pea Ridge, the Confederacy's interest in the Newtonia area was increased, not just for lead and land but for the purpose

45

of gaining more control and presence in Missouri.

The most strategic and useful attractions in the small town was the house, barn, mill, land, and rock fences, owned by Matthew H. Ritchey, a northern sympathizer but slaveholder, who was a paymaster for the Union army. Ritchey first came to the area from Overton, Tennessee, in the spring of 1832 in a steer-drawn covered wagon, settling and founding the village of Ritchey, Missouri, a few miles north of Newtonia. He farmed the bottom land along Shoal Creek, married Polly King and had ten children. He was elected constable in 1836 and went on to serve as County Judge, representative to the state legislature, and as a state senator. During the Civil War, Ritchey was Captain of the State Militia and a delegate to the State Convention, called to decide on the issue of Missouri's secession from the Union.[1]

The brick two-story Ritchey home, known as the Newtonia Civil War Mansion (or the Ritchey Mansion House), was built, ironically, using slave labor. The bricks were made from clay dug and fired on the property, and the house was completed in the summer of 1844.[2] The home was commandeered and served as a headquarters and hospital for both the Union and the Confederates during the War Between the States. Ritchey's land, mill and spring, provided food and water for livestock and the multitude of troops; and the large stone barn and vast stone fencing, provided a breastworks and ample cover for troops posted on the plantation-type property. All the Ritchey buildings received damage as a result of the battles waged in Newtonia - by artillery and gunfire.

The closest Union commander to Newtonia, at the time, was Brigadier General Frederick Salomon who was encamped at Sarcoxie about 12 miles to the north with an army of about 5,000 to 6,000 men. On September 29, 1862, he ordered Colonel Edward Lynde to take a scouting party of about 150 men to see what the Confederates were doing in that area. After a skirmish with some of Confederate Colonel Joseph O. Shelby's men, killing two and capturing one,[3] they withdraw, but by the next morning they were reinforced by Colonel

Jacobi's Wisconsin infantry, Kansas cavalry, and a force of Pin Indians. They began their attack early in the morning against the Confederates at Newtonia.

The town was crawling with a superior Southern force, consisting of Colonel Shelby's brigade of over 2,000, and about 200 Texans under Colonel Trezevant C. Hawpe.[4] Concerning Shelby and his brigade of Missouri cavalry, Colonel Thomas L. Snead, C.S.A., wrote that he was "one of the very best officers I have ever known. The men had all just been recruited in Missouri, and were as fine a body of young fellows as ever fought under any flag."[5] However, in command at Newtonia on account of his seniority, was Confederate Colonel Douglas H. Cooper who had 4,000 to 5,000 Cherokees, Choctaws, and half-breeds under Lieutenant Colonel Tandy Walker.[6] It was Colonel Hiram Miller Bledsoe (Old "Hi" Bledsoe), who was in command of the artillery in the town. Bledsoe will long be remembered by Civil War enthusiasts for his favorite gun called "Old Sacramento,"[7] a cannon that was captured during the Mexican War in 1847 at the Battle of Sacramento while Bledsoe was serving with Alexander W. Doniphan's "famous cavalry, whose prodigious marches and dashing combats adorn the brightest pages of American history."[8]

The old magnificent Mexican fieldpiece was thought to have been cast and smelted from Chihuahua brass church bells, and a quantity of silver in the mix. When the Mexican War was over, Doniphan brought the cannon and several others relics back to Missouri river-towns, so they could continue to echo their heroic tales of the past by being fired at Fourth of July celebrations and such. It was Bledsoe who fired Old Sacramento at events held at Lexington, Missouri.

When the Civil War broke out Bledsoe naturally drafted his cannon into Confederate service. The ancient 9-pounder was then bored out into a 12-pound howitzer. "The chase was turned off smooth, thus reducing the thickness of the metal, which gave the piece a peculiar sound when fired...."[9] It was said that he loved his old Mexican cannon so much that he was seen occasionally kissing its hand-polished barrel as a sign of his affections for it.[10]

Keeping Shelby in the background, Cooper sent his Indian warriors whooping loudly into Lynde and Jacobi and drove them away from Newtonia about six miles distance.[11] Before long, however, Salomon's main force arrived in the afternoon to aid and renew the fighting. After taking control of the high ground west of town, Salomon opened up a thunderous bombardment of cannon fire from his two six-gun batteries. From the strategic breastworks at Newtonia on Matthew Ritchey's farm, Bledsoe poured out his own death dealing cannonade toward the Federal position until the ammunition was exhausted.[12]

In an attempt to flank the Confederates at Newtonia, Salomon sent the Ninth Wisconsin German troops to circle around the town, which forced the Texans to fall back under their heavy gunfire. As a result, Cooper ordered up Shelby's Missourians under Lieutenant Colonel Gordon to ride in and rescue Hawpe's Texans, who put the German infantry to flight.[13]

In an all out Confederate onslaught of red and white soldiers, after the battle had raged for several hours, Salomon's army of Federals were defeated and driven from the battleground and forced to retreat in the darkness to grope their way back to Sarcoxie. About the action, Cooper reported that their guns and bayonets could be seen glistening in the sun as the mass of infantry advanced in superb order. "The booming of cannons, the bursting of shells, the air filled with missiles of every description, the rattling crash of small arms, the cheering of our men, and the war-whoops of our Indian allies, all combined to render the scene both grand and terrific."[14]

The Confederates had won the battle at Newtonia, but about the Indians who fought there, Annie Heloise Abel, in her book *The American Indian as Participant in the Civil War*, wrote: "Their discipline had yet left much to be desired. Scalping of the dead took place as on the battle-field of Pea

Ridge; but, in other respects, the Indians of both armies acquitted themselves well and far better than might have been expected.

"The participation of the Indian in the Battle of Newtonia was significant. Federals and Confederates had alike resorted to it for purposes other than the red man's own."[15] Union casualties at the 1st Battle of Newtonia were about 245 killed, wounded or missing; while the Confederate casualties were about 78 killed, wounded or missing.[16]

The prize that Cooper had gained at Newtonia at the Ritchey plantation farm, however, would be short-lived. In just a few days "the Federals were greatly reinforced and, in the first days of October, Schofield and Blunt, who had both arrived recently upon the scene, coming to the aid of Salomon, who had been the vanquished one at Newtonia, were able, in combination with Totten, to deprive Cooper of all the substantial fruits of victory."[17]

Blunt pursued Cooper into Arkansas and camped on the old Pea Ridge battlefield. In a few days they would come to blows just inside Indian Territory west of Maysville, Arkansas, at old Fort Wayne where Indian troops of both sides would again face each other in war.

Chapter 8

Capturing Old Fort Wayne

The methods and habits of warfare exercised by the Indians in conjunction with the warring armies at the Battle of Pea Ridge and 1st Newtonia, left Union and Confederate commands with the alternative decision of confining the Indian troops, for the most part, to their own territory. Soon after Pea Ridge this sentiment was already being expressed and acted upon, the Indians, according to author Annie Heloise Abel, "were regarded as distinctly inferior. Pea Ridge was, in fact, the first and last time that they were allowed to participate in the war on a big scale. Henceforth, they were rarely ever more than scouts and skirmishers and that was all they were really fitted to be."[1]

D.H. Maury, Assistant Adjutant-General, wrote to

Brigadier General Albert Pike on March 21, 1862, about the role his Indian troops would be expected to perform in their own territory in the future, saying: "...It is not expected that you will give battle to a large force, but by felling trees, burning bridges, removing supplies of forage and subsistence, attacking his trains, stampeding his animals, cutting off his detachments, and other similar means, you will be able materially to harass his army...please endeavor to restrain them from committing any barbarities upon the wounded, prisoners, or dead who may fall into their hands...."[2]

Regardless of how they felt about the Indians suitability in the armed conflict, they did nevertheless continue to participate in Civil War battles, but primarily in the Indian Nations. However, after receiving orders from General James S. Rains to attempt an invasion to molest Kansas, Cooper's Confederate Indians were camped at old Fort Wayne making plans for that mission; but Union General James G. Blunt under orders from General Schofield was marching to defeat Cooper, spoil his plans, and gain the "undisputed possession of Indian Territory north of the Arkansas [River]."[3]

On a hill overlooking the Illinois River in present-day Watts, Oklahoma, in Adair County, is the site of Camp Illinois, also known as Fort Wayne, which was began October 29, 1838, by Lieutenant Colonel Richard B. Mason, 1st Dragoons, U.S. Army, after residents of Arkansas expressed their fears and concerns over the proximity of the Cherokees who had just been relocated to the area. In 1839 work on the fort was halted when several soldiers became seriously sick and died, including Captain John Stuart, 7th Infantry.[4]

As a result, the decision was made to abandon the project and move it to the north side of Spavinaw (Flag) Creek, in present-day Delaware County, Oklahoma, just west of Maysville, Arkansas, in the autumn of 1839. The post, once again dubbed Fort Wayne in honor of General "Mad" Anthony Wayne of Revolutionary War fame, was established in June 1840 by Lieutenant Colonel Richard B. Mason, 1st Dragoons.[5]

Constructed in an area known as Beatie's Prairie, Fort

Wayne, was intended as only one in a series of forts that would safeguard the military road which was planned to run from Fort Snelling, Minnesota, to Fort Towson in southeastern Indian Territory (Oklahoma). However, by May 26, 1842, the War Department decided to abandon it to concentrate on the establishment of Fort Scott in southeastern Kansas. Early on in the Civil War the Confederacy took an interest in the log barracks and two rows of stone pillboxes at abandoned Fort Wayne, so Cherokee Colonel Stand Watie began to recruit and organize his Cherokee Mounted Rifles there in July 1861.[6] At last, the land and property of Fort Wayne was eventually put under the control of the Department of the Interior on March 26, 1871, its usefulness had finally come to an end.[7]

But on the night of October 21, 1862, it was a different story, Blunt was marching his troops in hot pursuit of Cooper towards Beatie's Prairie and Fort Wayne with the hope of catching his Indian force there unaware. General Cooper, being forewarned of their intentions, was ready to fall back in the event of their opponents arrival.[8]

At dawn, October 22, 1862, Blunt ordered the attack with only three small companies of cavalry, intending to keep Cooper's army in check until the rest of his Federals on the double quick could join the assault. Cooper, taking note of the small size of the attacking force, counterattacked on both of Blunt's flanks hoping to squeeze the Federals. After the arrival of a Kansas regiment with two cannon, a savage battle of dueling artillery ensued. Then, after the arrival of the 6th Kansas Cavalry reinforcing the right, and Colonel Phillips' 3rd Indian Home Guard on the left, the Confederate movement was put down. Five Federal cavalry companies then plunged into the heart of the Confederate center and captured their four-gun battery.[9]

Finally, with Blunt's entire force now on the field, Cooper's Indians were "greatly outnumbered...a demoralized host"[10] and forced to retreat "by way of Fort Gibson across the Arkansas River to Cantonment Davis, Stand Watie and his doughty Cherokees covering their retreat."[11] The Union pursued the defeated Southerners as far as Spavinaw Creek the day they captured old Fort Wayne.

In a few months the largest and most significant battle ever waged in Indian Territory would be fought, which came to be known by some as the "Gettysburg of Indian Territory." The battle would help insure the Union's control of northern Indian Territory for the remainder of the Civil War.

Chapter 9

A Gettysburg with War Paint

While the Civil War was continuing to draw inconceivable amounts of blood in the east, an important major battle was also brewing in the west in Indian Territory. At stake, and vulnerable, was Fort Gibson which had been recaptured by the Union April 5, 1863, with the help of Cherokee volunteers. And so, the Confederacy wanted it back. About twenty miles to the south of Fort Gibson, at a place known as Honey Springs (a supply depot and base of operations established by the Confederates in the spring of 1863), Confederate General Douglas H. Cooper was stationed there that summer with plans to attack and lay siege to the object of his affections - Fort Gibson.

The fort was first established on April 21, 1824, by Colonel Matthew Arbuckle, 7th Infantry, and was also known as Cantonment Davis and Fort Blunt. It was located on the

Grand River above Three Forks, where the Grand, Verdigris, and Arkansas rivers converge. Fort Gibson was originally founded to keep Osage Indian hostilities in check, and for the sake of military and exploratory expeditions. By 1857 the fort was deserted, but at the outbreak of the War Between the States it reclaimed its usefulness to the Confederates, until it was retaken by the Union. It was eventually abandoned and turned over to the Interior Department on February 7, 1891; and in 1936 much of Fort Gibson went through a restoration as a historical landmark.[1]

The coming battle of Honey Springs, to detour the Confederates away from Fort Gibson, also cut deep into the very heart of the Indians initial enthusiasm. "In the fortunes of the Southern Indians, the Battle of Honey Springs was a decisive event. Fought and lost in the country of the Creeks, it was bound to have upon them a psychological effect disastrous to the steady maintenance of their alliance with the Confederacy, so also with the other great tribes; but more of that anon. In a military way, it was no less significant than in a political; for it was the beginning of a vigorously offensive campaign, conducted by General Blunt, that never ended until the Federals were in occupation of Fort Smith [Arkansas] and Fort Smith was at the very door of the Choctaw country. No Indian tribe, at the outset of the war, had more completely gone over to the South than had the Choctaw...."[2]

In July 1863 during the hot scorching days of the summer season General Blunt arrived at Fort Gibson with about 600 men and two pieces of artillery, and was presently informed of General Cooper's Texans and Indians encamped to the south on Elk Creek near Honey Springs. Blunt was given orders to prepare to cross the Arkansas River and attack Cooper's post on the Texas Road, before Cooper could be reinforced for his own planned raid on Fort Gibson.[3]

Meanwhile, General William L. Cabell, with an Arkansas cavalry brigade and four artillery pieces were marching from Fort Smith, Arkansas, to join up with Cooper for their play on Fort Gibson. A Union victory for Blunt could depend upon his attack on Cooper coming before Cabell's arrival.

Blunt spent July 16 moving his 3,000 troops across the Arkansas River and forming them into two brigades. In one of these brigades at Honey Springs were the First Kansas Colored Infantry, who would gain the historical distinction of being in the first Civil War battle where African Americans proved their undisputed worth as brave fighting soldiers. It was written that "after that battle no one on either side in that section could be heard to say, 'Colored soldiers will not fight.' Thus was a prejudice of long standing wiped out in a few hours."[4] One African American man reported that: "...he frequently heard Southern officers, talking with each other, say that they did not believe colored soldiers would fight, and that all the Southern troops would have to do would be to march up to the colored men and take them in. The belief that colored soldiers would not fight was not at that time confined to Southern officers, but a good many Federal officers and people in the North expressed the same sentiment, particularly those who were opposed to enlisting colored men for soldiers in the Union army."[5] However, before the battle, it was reported that scouts had brought word that no quarter would be given to any of the First Kansas Colored Infantry, which might have explained the ferocity of their fighting that summer day at Honey Springs. For whatever the reasons, their hard-fought contribution was undoubtedly great.

Also making the attack with Blunt, besides the 1st Kansas Colored Infantry, was the 1st Indian Home Guards, 2nd Indian Home Guards, 6th Kansas Cavalry, 3rd Wisconsin Cavalry, Smith's Battery, 2nd Colorado Infantry, Hopkin's Kansas Battery, and the 3rd Indian Home Guards.[6]

Just north of the Honey Springs depot deployed along both sides of the Texas Military Road were about 5,000 of Cooper's Confederates, consisting of the 20th Texas Cavalry, 29th Texas Cavalry, 5th Texas Partisan Rangers, Lee's Light Battery, Colonel Tandy Walker's war-painted 1st Choctaw and Chickasaw Mounted Rifles, Colonel Stand Watie's 1st and 2nd Cherokee Mounted Rifles, a squadron of Texas Cavalry, and the 1st and 2nd Creek Cavalry under Colonel D.N. McIntosh.[7]

On the morning of July 17, 1863, after a shower of rain fell which reportedly left the Confederate's Mexican gunpowder a gooey worthless paste, the Federals opened up with a deafening and roaring round of cannon fire followed by a storm of screaming hot musket lead. The Confederates returned the favor with a desperate hurricane of shot, shell, and exploding canister, but soon had to fall back down the Texas Road to a position Cooper had pre-selected, if it became necessary, in the trees along Elk Creek.[8]

Quickly the Federals moved forward and resumed the bitter contest for several more hours, and at one point the Confederates "came up within twenty-five yards of the colored regiment, who gave them a volley of musketry, shooting down their color-bearer, besides killing and wounding a number of other men and quickly sending the others back in considerable confusion. Their colors were again raised, but in a few moments were shot down again by the volleys from the colored infantry and left to fall into the hands of the Federal forces by the retreating Texans...."[9]

Eventually, Cooper's Southerners were forced to retreat south of Elk Creek over a bridge they tried to no avail to hold for a time, "but the troops defending them were speedily driven from these positions by the Federal infantry and the guns of Captain Hopkin's battery, which had moved forward and taken up the position which had just been occupied by the guns of the Confederate battery...."[10]

After the Confederate troops had hightailed it from the Honey Springs area heading south, Blunt's victorious Union troops offered chase for a short while as Cooper's rearguard cavalry units covered their retreat. Blunt found that Cooper's men had hastily torched their warehouses of supplies at the depot in order to keep them from falling into the hands of the Yankees. However, one commissary building was spared from the fire, which contained a fair amount of bacon, flour, salt, and dried beef, that the battle-weary Northerners quickly utilized for their own nightly supper on the Honey Springs battleground.[11]

The Union troops remained until the next evening giving aid to "the wounded and burying the dead of both sides." Blunt reported that his losses were 17 killed and 60 wounded; and he reported Confederate losses to be 150 killed and 400 wounded[12] at the Battle of Honey Springs (or Elk Creek), which is located near present-day Rentiesville, Oklahoma.

As for General Cabell who was en route to Cooper from Fort Smith, he was within two hours of witnessing the end of the battle and could hear the booming and thunder of their cannons in the distance. Helplessly, Cabell's two thousand soldiers finally joined up with Cooper too late to help reverse the outcome of the battle, and retired together south of the Canadian River.[13]

Within a few weeks after the clash at Honey Springs General Blunt occupied Fort Smith, and a large part of Indian Territory was now under Union control. However, Colonel Stand Watie continued his vigorous reign of terror against the Union, raiding north of the Arkansas River many times and inflicting severe damage to Federal supply bases - always eluding capture by his formidable wiles.

So far, Native Americans, wanting only to live in peace, raise their families, and hunt on the land they had come to love even as their forefathers, received only one death dealing situation added to the next. From the crackling firesides of their contentment, to the raging unwanted din of a bloody battle some have called the "Gettysburg of Indian Territory," these peoples continue their trek of life with the simple hope and passion of a more certain future void of pain. But, unfortunately, there would be more turmoil ahead in the birth pangs of an ever changing nation - and more deaths as well. At one such place in southern Arkansas, they would be supping up more of the same at a battle known as Poison Spring.

Chapter 10

Foraging Mule Train

In April 1864 Union and Confederates would again be pitted against each other in a significant battle in southern Arkansas, where Native Americans would again leave Indian Territory and join in the first encounter of what is known as the Camden Expedition of Union Major General Frederick Steele. The expedition, which was to occur in conjunction with the Red River Campaign of Union Major General Nathaniel P. Banks under orders from Lieutenant General Ulysses S. Grant, were to eventually converge on the Southerners in Louisiana. The Confederates, under Major General Sterling Price, were expecting such an expedition and had seen to it that the entire area was void of forage, which made the attack and interruption of a U.S. supply train of about 200 wagons at Poison Spring a serious problem for the Federal troops who desperately needed the valuable cargo to operate in the area militarily.[1]

The foraging mule train left Camden, Arkansas, on April

17 under the care of Union Colonel James M. Williams, along with a 695 troop escort consisting of the First Kansas Colored Infantry (who fought at 1st Cabin Creek and Honey Springs), the Second Kansas Cavalry Regiment, Sixth Kansas Cavalry Regiment, 14th Kansas Cavalry, and the Second Indiana Battery. However, Williams was reinforced on the morning of the 18th by the 18th Iowa Infantry Regiment and others, which brought his escort force to about 1,000 men.[2]

General Price's force consisted of about 3,700 men and twelve artillery pieces with Brigadier General John S. Marmaduke on the right, Brigadier General William L. Cabell in the center, and Brigadier General Samuel B. Maxey's Texans of Colonel Richard Gano and the Choctaw and Chickasaw Indians under Colonel Tandy Walker on the left flank; each division would have a four gun battery making up their centers.[3]

The area of battle at Poison Spring was described as having "twenty to thirty acres in it, and the north end of it was about two hundred yards south of the Camden road. Nearly all the high ground in that section not in cultivation was covered with pine timber, and in some places with a young growth of pine, making it impossible to see objects more than a hundred yards or so in front."[4] After shots were fired to determine the strength and location of the enemy at Poison Spring, the Confederates responded and "opened a heavy cross-fire of shot and shell upon the Federal line,"[5] which lasted about half an hour. During the bombardment an African American soldier of the 1st Kansas Colored Infantry was struck between his shoulders, and as a result of his outbursts of agony gave away the Federal position. A cyclone of shot and shell was quickly directed by the Confederates, and after the cannonade ceased volleys of buck and ball from infantrymen followed. It was said that the lines of battle came so close to each other it was reported that the 29th Texas, who hadn't forgotten their defeat at Honey Springs where the 1st Kansas Colored Infantry had participated, called out and said: "You First Nigger, now buck to the Twenty-ninth Texas."[6]

Colonel Williams was learning rapidly that the cause of protecting his mule train of foraged supplies was not going to be an easy one. He hoped that the deafening roar of the big guns would alert reinforcements from Camden, a few miles to the north. General Steele heard the cannons at Poison Spring but did not order any further troops to their aid.[7]

After the Confederates had assaulted Colonel Williams' lines four times with many of them killed and wounded, "the colored infantry were forced from their position back to the rear of the train and formed on the left of the Eighteenth Iowa, pouring volley after volley into the lines of the exulting foe as they retired.

"The Federal troops and train were now entirely surrounded, and the firing of small-arms and artillery, the crashing of shot and bursting shell in among the teams of the large train, the roar of the battle, and the shouting of the victorious Confederate troops soon caused a scene of great confusion."[8]

About Walker's Indians and their contribution, it was said that: "The Choctaws under Tandy Walker were found quite willing to cross the line and they did excellent service in the Camden campaign, which, both in the cannonade near Prairie d' Ane on the thirteenth of April and in the Battle of Poison Spring on the eighteenth of April, offered a thorough test of what Indians could do when well disciplined, well officered, and well considered. The Indian reinforcement of Marmaduke was ungrudgingly given and ungrudgingly commended."[9]

What was left of Colonel Williams' exhausted force was marched through the swamps and the Arkansas pines, until they reached the safety of Camden that night. The Confederates pursued for a time but, broke off the chase for fear of Union reinforcements that might be stationed at Camden.

The poor souls of the 1st Kansas Colored Infantry who fought hard in the past and again at Poison Spring, suffered at the hands of the Southern victors. The 2nd Indian Brigade turned to lifting scalps, while the Texans full of rage, revenge, and even racism, also had some unsavory pay back to perform on the African Americans who were left behind on the battleground that day; they also suffered in other ways. "Some who were too badly wounded to walk, lay on the field, and when the Confederates came near them, feigned being dead, and crawled off the field after dark, and endeavored to make their way back to camp, marching while they had strength and then lying down in the grass and weeds to rest. Several colored soldiers who were badly wounded, and who from weakness and loss of blood were obliged to march and rest at intervals, were bitten by poisonous snakes while lying down in the grass or weeds during the night, and when they got into camp the next day their bodies were horribly swollen from the effect of the poison which had spread through their systems. One of the colored soldiers who was wounded and lay on the field until night feigning death, and then crawled off and made his way into camp, stated that he saw the Confederates shooting the wounded colored soldiers who were left on the field, and that Confederate soldiers went over the field after the battle, calling out and answering each other, 'Where is the First Nigger now?' 'All cut to pieces and gone to hell by bad management.'"[10]

Consider, that at this point in history, the institution of slavery and other customs and traditions were common place in American society, and according to the New Testament, it reads: "Servants, be subject to your masters with all fear; not only to the good and gentle, but also to the froward."[11] And again: "Servants, be obedient to them that are your masters according to the flesh, with fear and trembling in singleness of your heart, as unto Christ."[12] And: "Let as many servants as are under the yoke count their own masters worthy of all honor...."[13]

The Federal foraging mule train, artillery, and other captured supplies, were quickly confiscated by the Confederates at Poison Spring and added to their own war efforts. The Camden Expedition and Red River Campaign of the Union was derailed like a train, and on April 19, the day after the Battle of Poison Spring, Major General Edmund Kirby-Smith arrived with 8,000 more Southern troops to take command in Arkansas.[14]

Federal losses as a result of the battle at Poison Spring left 122 killed, 97 wounded, and 81 reported missing. The 1st Kansas Colored Infantry lost 117 killed, and 65 wounded. The Confederate casualties were 17 killed, 88 wounded, and 10 unaccounted for.

Chapter 11

Stand Watie's Victory

On May 10, 1864, while camped at the Cherokee headquarters in the Choctaw Nation, Indian Territory, a courier arrived with news from Confederate President Jefferson Davis that Colonel Stand Watie was promoted to Brigadier General. As the exciting word spread among his loyal Cherokee followers of the 1st and 2nd Regiments, the camp exploded in celebration as his men marched around his tent to the sound of the drum and the fife.[1] Their wily leader, known as the "red fox," had achieved something extraordinary for all of them, by becoming the only Native American in any army North or South to attain such a rank.

Before long, Brigadier General Watie received orders to take his 1st Indian Brigade of 800 men and join up with Brigadier General Richard M. Gano's Texas Brigade of 1,200 men, and travel north of Fort Gibson to the Grand and

Neosho river valley and engage the Federals. The Confederate plan was to sidetrack and occupy the Union army, so that Major General Sterling Price could more easily invade Missouri with the help of the diversion.[2]

In early September Watie and Gano's combined force, 2,000 strong, were about twelve miles north of Fort Gibson on the west side of Grand River when their scouts came across a Federal hay camp at a place known as Flat Rock. African Americans of the 1st Kansas Colored Infantry were scattered over the area cutting and putting up prairie hay. Also in the camp were two Federal detachments of the 2nd Kansas Cavalry under Captain E.A. Barker - in all about 125 men guarding the hay.[3]

The hayfield area where Barker was working his men had other interesting features as well, and was said that: "His camp was nearly two miles from Grand River timber, on a prairie branch along which, every hundred yards or so, there were pools or lagoons from a few yards to fifty yards long, and in places perhaps two feet deep, and connected by narrow treads of water. The low banks of the lagoon were generally precipitous or caving, with overhanging boughs of small willows. In some of them there were numerous water-lilies, with their large palm-like leaves floating on the surface."[4]

The Confederates attacked and burned 5,000 tons of hay, wagons and mowing machines. Captain Barker managed to somehow repel several Confederate cavalry charges from his position, and his mounted men eventually broke through the Federal line to safety but, left stranded men of the 1st Colored Infantry under Lieutenant Thomas B. Sutherland. The Confederates showed little mercy at Flat Rock as, "...the colored soldiers were pursued and shot down without any demand for their surrender." One "colored soldier jumped into a lagoon which was deep enough to conceal his body, and managed by lying on his back to expose enough of his nose above the water under the overhanging willows to breathe freely."[5] The merciless massacre at Flat Rock ended when there were no longer any more defenseless victims to be found, and the Confederates spent the night on the bloody ground where the outnumbered unfortunate hay cutters had worked.

Near present-day Pensacola, Oklahoma, at a place called Cabin Creek, two battles were fought during the Civil War. The area was important to the Union and the Confederates because it was the site of a stockade built by the Union in 1863, which was on the Fort Scott-Fort Gibson Military Road atop a bluff overlooking Cabin Creek. The road, also known as the Immigrant Road to Texas or the Texas Road, was first an ancient Indian trace used by the Osage and became a path for settlers heading for their new lives in the west.[6]

In June 1863 Union General James G. Blunt and a long supply train was attacked by then Colonel Stand Watie at Cabin Creek. Watie's Southern lines, who were on the opposite side of the swollen creek, were routed by Blunt's men. Watie suffered his worst defeat in the 1st Battle of Cabin Creek.[7]

However, in the early morning hours of September 19, 1864, three days after the massacre at Flat Rock, Captain Henry Hopkins in command of a 300-wagon Federal supply train en route to Fort Gibson, was camped at Cabin Creek stockade. Hopkins' train was guarded by the 2nd Kansas Cavalry, detachments of the 6th and 14th Kansas Cavalry, and the 2nd and 3rd Indian Home Guard - in all about 600 men.[8]

Meanwhile, the Confederates commanded by Brigadier General Gano, because his commission predated Watie's by about one month, having learned of the wagon train at Cabin Creek, were forming for battle. Gano had the 29th, 30th, and 31st Texas Cavalry, and Howell's six gun battery; while Watie had the 1st and 2nd Cherokee Mounted Rifles, the 1st and 2nd Creek, and a Seminole Battalion - a total of about 2,000 men.[9]

About 2 o'clock a.m. the Confederate artillery split the darkness and stillness of the night with their lightning flashes of black powder and an earsplitting blaze of shot and shell, followed by the hair raising battle cries of Gano and Watie's bloodthirsty Indians and Texans, as they made their advance on the Union supply train and encampment. With the stockade almost surrounded by the war whooping Confederates, the Federals were pressed and had only the steep bluff behind them that ran sharply down to the creek below. With their backs to the wall, the firing from both sides continued until daylight, when: "...an incessant storm of shot and bursting shell swept through the camp and train, killing and wounding many of the mules, stampeding the teams, and causing inextricable entanglement in the absence of the teamsters. The bluff that rose almost abruptly from the creek in the rear of the camp, the stockade, and a narrow ravine on the Federal right afforded much protection to the Federal soldiers during this terrible artillery fire."[10]

Many of the mule teams became panic stricken and dragged many wagons over the bluff's edge 100 feet to the creek bed below, overturning and breaking them into pieces. By 9:00 that morning the battle was over, and Watie and Gano claimed their booty at the 2nd Battle of Cabin Creek; Stand Watie had finally gained his payback victory. All of the remaining wagons, about 130 of them, were seized by the Confederates. "This was the most serious disaster the Federal forces met with in the Indian Territory during the war."[11]

The battle at Cabin Creek was the last major engagement in the Indian Nations, and for their efforts gained - 130 wagons heavily loaded with a vast quantity of commissary supplies and war materials - and 740 mules for their triumphant return trip south. The stockade was burned to the ground, along with about 3,000 tons of hay and the equipment. The captured train, at the time, was said to be worth over $1,500,000, which went a long way in helping the destitute Confederate Indians continue their cause during the final days of the War of the Rebellion.[12]

Many of the casualties of the Cabin Creek battle lie buried in unmarked and forgotten graves. Union casualties were reported to be about 54 killed, wounded or missing. Confederate numbers were about 45 killed, wounded or missing.[13]

On June 23, 1865, Stand Watie, the hard riding and hard fighting warrior of Indian Territory reluctantly surrendered. With tears welling up in his eyes, his command and commission as a Brigadier General of the Confederate States of American, was over.

Author's
Final Word

At the end of the great Civil War the territories that had become home away from home to many Native Americans, was left in ruins. Where they again faced disease, starvation, and misery, in a land of blackened fields and forests and burned out homes and schools. From the east they were forced to march on with fear and uncertainty in the foreign grasp of cruelty, only to again find the same all to familiar tears revisit them once more in the west.

The thunderous sounds of massive moving herds of buffalo, replaced by the sonic booms of jet airplanes and the constant rolling of big eighteen wheelers. Vast lands and open range lush and teeming with life and abundant game, crowded out by robust construction and a sea of concrete; but the wild and free natural beauty that was the Native American heart and experience, remains forever a nostalgic reality of American history.

The participation of the Indian in the War Between the States, which occurred in the western theater of war, is little known to most but as important to the American story as any of the Civil War. Their blood that was spilled was as red as any and just as real. Their losses were felt by their own loved ones just the same as they are with any race of people. And so their sacrifice just as great.

Acknowledgements

I would like to thank my wife Katherine for being such a large part of everything at home, and in the field, while making this book. Thanks to my three sons Ryan, Seth, and Eli, for all of their special contributions. I would also like to acknowledge my father, Ernest J. Jackson, who died in the fall of 1998 and continues to inspire me with his words of wisdom and guidance, even more. I am also grateful to Scott Sallee and everyone at the Blue & Gray magazine.

Thanks to the Neosho, Missouri, Newton County Library. Also, thanks goes to all of the authors and publishers for much of the information used in this book, the work would not have been possible to do without it.

A debt of gratitude is also offered to Leslie Wolfinger, Corinne Will, Karen Ackermann, Lisa Loveless, Debbie Riley, and everyone at Heritage Books and Willow Bend Books, who work on and behind the scenes to further publish and make available such important history.

Finally, thanks to all of the Native Americans for the sacrifices they made for the country they loved.

The likeness of Stand Watie carved in stone at the Old Ridge-Poison
Cemetery near Southwest City, Missouri, in
Delaware County, Oklahoma.
(Photo by the author)

Monument to Stand Watie at the Old Ridge-Poison Cemetery.
(Photo by the author)

The Old Ridge-Poison Cemetery.
(Author's photo)

The final resting place of Confederate Brigadier General Stand Watie
at the Old Ridge-Poison Cemetery.
(Author's photo)

Gravesite of Major Ridge at the Old Ridge-Poison Cemetery, principle
leader of the Ridge Party before his assassination, June 22, 1839.
(Author's photo)

Headstone of John Ridge, son of Major Ridge, at the Old Ridge-Poison Cemetery. Also assassinated June 22, 1839.
(Author's photo)

A memorial to Chief John Ross, chief of the Ross Party, at the
Cherokee Heritage Center in Tahlequah, Oklahoma.
(Author's photo)

Cornerstone of Missouri, Arkansas, and Oklahoma, near
Southwest City, Missouri.
(Author's collection)

Civil War reenactment photo.
(Photo by the author)

Reenactment photo of Union and Confederate soldiers in fierce battle.
(Photo by the author)

A silent cannon at Wilson's Creek National Civil War Battlefield
near Springfield, Missouri.
(Photo by the author)

The historic Ray House at the Wilson's Creek National Civil War Battlefield. The home of John Ray, a slaveholder and Union loyalist at the time of the battle, where he watched the entire bloody conflict unfold from the vantage point of his front porch.
(Photo by the author)

The spot, presumably, near where Union Brigadier General Nathaniel Lyon fell in the Battle of Wilson's Creek, August 10, 1861, which was called the "Bloody Point."
(Author's photo)

EAGLE HOTEL

On the morning of March 6, 1862, Gen. Franz Sigel was eating his breakfast at the Eagle Hotel which stood on this site. He had remained here with 600 men and a battery of six pieces after the main column of his army had passed through Bentonville on its way to the camp on Sugar Creek. Confederate troops under Gen. Van Dorn surprised him and forced a hasty retreat. In 1887 Sigel returned to retrace his route and remarked that he had come back to finish his breakfast.

Site of the Eagle Hotel in Bentonville, Arkansas, where Union General Franz Sigel was eating his breakfast on the morning of March 6, 1862. (Author's collection)

The Elkhorn Tavern at the Pea Ridge National Civil War
Battlefield, Pea Ridge, Arkansas.
(Photo by the author)

The Elkhorn Tavern, Pea Ridge National Civil War Battlefield.
(Author's photo)

Historic marker at the Pea Ridge National Civil War Battlefield on the
Old Butterfield Overland Mail Stagecoach Route.
(Author's photo)

Now silent at the Pea Ridge National Civil War Battlefield, is this
artillery battery near Elkhorn Tavern.
(Photo by the author)

The Ritchey Civil War Mansion at Newtonia, Missouri.
(Photo by the author)

Final resting place of Confederate Colonel Hiram Miller Bledsoe at the
Pleasant Hill Cemetery, Pleasant Hill, Missouri, who was
famous for Bledsoe's Battery.
(Author's photo)

OKLAHOMA

FORT WAYNE

ESTABLISHED IN 1838 BY LT. COL. R.B. MASON, 1ST DRAGOONS, U.S. ARMY, AT REQUEST OF ARKANSAS CITIZENS FEARING CHEROKEES WHO WERE BEING REMOVED FROM SOUTHEASTERN U.S. NAMED IN HONOR OF GEN. "MAD" ANTHONY WAYNE. THE FORT WAS ORIGINALLY LOCATED IN NE CORNER OF PRESENT-DAY WATTS ON A HILL OVERLOOKING ILLINOIS RIVER. CONSIDERED POOR LOCATION BECAUSE MANY SOLDIERS DIED THERE, INCLUDING CAPT. JOHN STUART, 7TH INFANTRY. IN 1839, FORT WAS ABANDONED AND MOVED TO BEATIE'S PRAIRIE WEST OF MAYSVILLE, ARKANSAS. THAT SITE ABANDONED IN 1842 AND TROOPS MOVED NORTH TO ESTABLISH FORT SCOTT, KANSAS.

OKLAHOMA HISTORICAL SOCIETY
65-1995

MANUFACTURED BY
WILLIS GRANITE PRODUCTS
GRANITE, OKLAHOMA

Memorial in Watts, Oklahoma, to the first site of Fort Wayne.
(Author's photo)

The Honey Springs Historic Civil War Battlefield near
Rentiesville, Oklahoma.
(Author's photo)

Site of the 1st and 2nd Battle of Cabin Creek near
Pensacola, Oklahoma.
(Author's photo)

Chapter
Notes

Chapter 1
Treaties and Depots
of Death

1. *Myths of the Cherokee,* by James Mooney, Nineteenth Annual Report of the U.S. Bureau of American Ethnology to the Secretary of the Smithsonian Institution 1900
2. Ibid.
3. Ibid.
4. *The Confederate Cherokee: John Drew's Regiment of Mounted Rifles,* by W. Craig Gaines, Louisiana State University Press, Baton Rouge and London 1989
5. Mooney
6. Ibid.
7. Gaines
8. Mooney
9. *Cherokee Tragedy: The Story of the Ridge Family and the Decimation of a people,* by Thurman Wilkins, The Macmillan Company, Collier Macmillan LTD., London 1970; Mooney
10. Mooney
11. Ibid.
12. Ibid.
13. Ibid.
14. *Bingham: Fighting Artist,* by Lew Larkin, Burton Publishing Company, Inc., Kansas City 1954
15. Mooney
16. Ibid.
17. Ibid.
18. Wilkins

Chapter 2
A Tearful Journey
to the Civil War

1. *Myths of the Cherokee,* by James Mooney, Nineteenth Annual Report of the U.S. Bureau of American Ethnology to the Secretary of the Smithsonian Institution 1900

2. Ibid.
3. Ibid.
4. Ibid.
5. *Cherokee Tragedy: The Story of the Ridge Family and the Decimation of a People,* by Thurman Wilkins, The Macmillan Company, Collier Macmillan LTD., London 1970; *The Confederate Cherokee: John Drew's Regiment of Mounted Rifles,* by Craig Gaines, Louisiana State University Press, Baton Rouge and London 1989
6. Mooney
7. Ibid; Gaines
8. Agent Stokes to Secretary of War, June 24, 1839; Mooney
9. Old Ridge-Polson Cemetery, Delaware County, Oklahoma, Historical Marker; History of McDonald County, McDonald County Library, Pineville, Missouri; Gaines; Mooney; *Stand Watie's Grave,* by Rex Jackson, Blue & Gray magazine, Vol. XX, Issue 2, 2002
10.McDonald County Records, McDonald County Library, Pineville, Missouri
11.Old Ridge-Polson Cemetery, Delaware County, Oklahoma, Historical Marker; Gaines
12.McDonald County Records, McDonald County Library, Pineville, Missouri; Historic Marker just west of Maysville, Arkansas
13.Historic Marker at the Old Ridge-Polson Cemetery just west of Southwest City, Missouri
14.Mooney; *Civil War in Indian Territory,* by Steve Cottrell, Pelican Publishing Company, Gretna, Louisiana 1995
15.Mooney
16. *Cherokee Nation,* Royce, Fifth Annual Report, Bureau of Ethnology 1888; Mooney

Chapter 3
Resistance is Futile

1. *The War of the Rebellion: Official Records of the Union and Confederate Armies,* Series 1, Volume 1, Washington: Government Printing Office 1880

2. *The War of the Rebellion: Official Records of the Union and Confederate Armies,* Series 1, Volume 3, Washington: Government Printing Office 1880
3. Ibid.
4. Ibid.
5. *Civil War in the Indian Territory,* by Steve Cottrell, Pelican Publishing Company, Gretna, Louisiana 1995
6. Editors footnote, *Wilson's Creek, and the Death of Lyon,* by William M. Wherry, Battles and Leaders of the Civil War, Vol. 1, The Century Company 1887
7. *Battles and Biographies of Missourians: Civil War Period of Our State,* by W.L. Webb, Kansas City, Missouri, Hudson-Kimberly Publishing Company 1900

Chapter 4
Early Southern
Victories

1. *Wilson's Creek, and the Death of Lyon,* by William M. Wherry, Battles and Leaders of the Civil War, Vol. 1, The Century Company 1887
2. *Battles and Biographies of Missourians: Civil War Period of Our State,* by W.L. Webb, Kansas City, Missouri, Hudson-Kimberly Publishing Company 1900
3. Wherry
4. *An Account of the Battle of Wilson's Creek, or Oak Hills,* by Holcombe & Adams, Springfield, Missouri: Dow & Adams Publishers 1883
5. Ibid.
6. Webb
7. Ibid.
8. *The First Year of the War in Missouri,* by Colonel Thomas L. Snead, Battles and Leaders of the Civil War, Vol. 1, The Century Company 1887
9. Webb
10. Holcombe & Adams
11. Ibid.

12. Ibid.
13. Ibid.

Chapter 5
Opothleyoholo's Stand

1. *Union and Confederate Indians in the Civil War,* by Wiley
   Britton, Battles and Leaders of the Civil War, Vol. 1, The
   Century Company 1887
2. *The War of the Rebellion: Official Records of the Union and
   Confederate Armies,* Series 1, Volume 8, Washington:
   Government Printing Office 1883
3. Ibid.
4. Ibid.
5. Britton
6. OR, Series 1, Vol. 8
7. Ibid.
8. Ibid.
9. Ibid.
10. *Oklahoma: A History of the Sooner State,* by Edwin C.
    McReynolds, Norman, Oklahoma, University of Oklahoma Press
    1954
11. OR, Series 1, Vol. 8
12. Ibid.

Chapter 6
Tomahawkers and Scalpers

1. *The Pea Ridge Campaign,* by Franz Sigel, Battles and Leaders of
   the Civil War, Vol. 1, The Century Company 1887
2. *War of the Rebellion: Official Records of the Union and
   Confederate Armies,* Series 1, Volume 8, Washington:
   Government Primting Office 1883
3. *Soldiers in War Paint,* by Wayne T. Walker, The West: True
   Stories of the Old West magazine, March 1967
4. Ibid; *The American Indian as Participant in the Civil War,* by
   Annie Heloise Abel, Arthur H. Clark Company, Cleveland 1919

5. OR, Series 1, Vol. 8
6. Ibid.
7. Abel
8. Walker
9. OR, Series 1, Vol. 8
10. Ibid.
11. Ibid.
12. Walker
13. *Battles and Biographies of Missourians: Civil War Period of Our State,* by W.L. Webb, Kansas City, Missouri, Hudson-Kimberly Publishing Company 1900
14.OR, Series 1, Vol. 8
15. Ibid.
16. *The Pea Ridge Campaign,* Sigel
17. OR, Series 1, Vol. 8

Chapter 7
Lead and Land

1. *Newtonia: Southwest Missouri's Historic Civil War Home,* by Rex Jackson, The Ozarks Mountaineer magazine, October 2000
2. Ibid.
3. *General Jo Shelby: Undefeated Rebel,* by Daniel O'Flaherty, The University of North Carolina Press, Chapel Hill and London 1954
4. Ibid.
5. *The Conquest of Arkansas,* by Thomas L. Snead, Battles and Leaders of the Civil War, Vol. 3, The Century Company 1887
6. O'Flaherty; Snead
7. O'Flaherty
8. *Battles and Biographies of Missourians: Civil War Period of Our State,* by W.L. Webb, Kansas City, Missouri, Hudson-Kimberly Publishing Company 1900
9. Ibid.
10. *Civil War on the Western Border 1854-1865,* by Jay Monaghan, Little, Brown and Company, Boston and Toronto 1955
11. *Civil War in the Ozarks,* by Phillip W. Steele and Steve Cottrell,

Pelican Publishing Company, Gretna, Louisiana 1993
12. O'Flaherty
13. Ibid.
14. OR, Series 1, Vol. 13
15. *The American Indian as Participant in the Civil War,* by Annie Heloise Abel, Arthur H. Clark Company, Cleveland 1919
16. *Civil War in the Indian Territory,* by Steve Cottrell, Pelican Publishing Company, Gretna, Louisiana 1995
15. Abel

Chapter 8
Capturing Old
Fort Wayne

1. *The American Indian as Participant in the Civil War,* by Annie Heloise Abel, Arthur H. Clark Company, Cleveland 1919
2. *The War of the Rebellion: Official Records of the Union and Confederate Armies,* Series 1, Volume 8, Washington: Government Printing Office 1883
3. Abel
4. Historic Marker, Watts, Oklahoma
5. Historic Marker, Maysville, Arkansas
6. Ibid; *Encyclopedia of Historic Forts,* by Robert B. Roberts, Macmillan Publishing Company, Incorporated 1987
7. Roberts
8. *Oklahoma: A History of the Sooner State,* by Edwin C. McReynolds, University of Oklahoma Press, Norman, Oklahoma 1954
9. Ibid.
10. Abel
11. Ibid.

Chapter 9
A Gettsburg
with War Paint

1. *Encyclopedia of Historic Forts,* by Robert B. Roberts, Macmillan

Publishing Company, Incorporated 1987

2. *The American Indians as Participant in the Civil War,* Annie Heloise Abel, Arthur H. Clark Company, Cleveland 1919

3. *Soldiers in War Part,* by Wayne T. Walker, The West: True Stories of the Old West magazine, March 1967; *The Civil War on the Border,* by Wiley Britton, Vol.2, G.P. Putnam's Sons, New York and London, The Knickerbocker Press 1899

4. Britton

5. Ibid.

6. Honey Springs Historic Battlefield; Britton

7. Ibid.

8. Walker

9. Britton

10. Ibid.

11. *Oklahoma: A History of the Sooner State,* by Edwin C. McReynolds, University of Oklahoma Press, Norman, Oklahoma 1954

12. Britton

13. Ibid.

Chapter 10
Foraging Mule Train

1. *Civil War Battles in the West,* by Dean A. Bohlender, edited by LeRoy H. Fischer, Journal of the West, Inc., Sunflower University Press, Manhattan, Kansas 1981

2. Ibid.

3. *The Civil War on the Border,* by Wiley Britton, Vol. 2, G.P. Putnam's Sons, New York and London, The Knickerbocker Press 1899

4. Ibid.

5. Ibid.

6. Ibid.

7. Bohlender; Britton

8. Britton

9. *The American Indians as Participant in the Civil War,* by Annie Heloise Abel, Arthur H. Clark Company, Cleveland 1919

10. Britton
11. 1 Peter 2:18; *Civil War in Indian Territory,* by Steve Cottrell, Pelican Publishing Company, Gretna, Louisiana 1995
12. Ephesians 6:5
13. 1 Timothy 6:1
14. Britton; Bohlender
15. Ibid.

Chapter 11
Stand Watie's
Victory

1. *Soldiers in War Paint,* by Wayne T. Walker, The West: True Stories of the Old West magazine, March 1967
2. Ibid.
3. *The Civil War on the Border,* by Wiley Britton, Vol. 2, G.P. Putnam's Sons, New York and London, The Knickerbocker Press 1899
4. Ibid.
5. Ibid.
6. *Last Raid at Cabin Creek,* by Steven L. Warren, Simitar Entertainment, Inc., Maple Plain, Minnesota 1992
7. Ibid.
8. Historic Markers, Cabin Creek Civil War Park, Pensacola, Oklahoma
9. Ibid.
10. Britton
11. Ibid.
12. Cabin Creek Civil War Park
13. Warren

Bibliography

Abel, Annie Heloise, *The American Indian as Participant in the Civil War,* Arthur H. Clark Company, Cleveland 1919

Bohlender, Dean A., *Civil War Battles in the West,* The Battle of Poison Spring, edited by LeRoy H. Fischer, Journal of the West, Inc., Sunflower University Press, Manhattan, Kansas 1981

Britton, Wiley, *The Civil War on the Border,* Vol. 2, G.P. Putnam's Sons, The Knickerbocker Press, New York and London 1899; *Union and Confederate Indians in the Civil War,* Battles and Leaders of the Civil War, Vol. 1, The Century Company 1887

Cottrell, Steve, *Civil War in the Indian Territory,* Pelican Publishing Company, Gretna, Louisiana 1995

Gaines, Craig W., *The Confederate Cherokee: John Drew's Regiment of Mounted Rifles,* Louisiana State University Press, Baton Rouge and London 1989

Holcombe & Adams, *An Account of the Battle of Wilson's Creek,* Missouri: Dow & Adams Publishers 1883

Jackson, Rex, *Newtonia: Southwest Missouri's Historic Civil War Home,* The Ozarks Mountaineer magazine, October 2000; *Stand Watie's Grave,* Blue & Gray magazine, Vol. XX, Issue 2, 2002

Larkin, Lew, *Bingham: Fighting Artist,* Burton Publishing Company, Inc., Kansas City 1954

McReynolds, Edwin C., *Oklahoma: A History of the Sooner State,*

111

University of Oklahoma Press, Norman, Oklahoma 1954

Monaghan, Jay, *Civil War on the Western Border 1854-1865*, Little, Brown and Company, Boston and Toronto 1955

Mooney, James, *Myths of the Cherokee*, Nineteenth Annual Report of the Bureau of American Ethnology to the Secretary of the Smithsonian Institution 1900

O'Flaherty, Daniel, *General Jo Shelby: Undefeated Rebel*, The University of North Carolina Press, Chapel Hill and London 1954

Roberts, Robert B., *Encyclopedia of Historic Forts*, Macmillan Publishing Company, Incorporated 1987

Royce, *Cherokee Nation*, Fifth Annual Report, Bureau of Ethnology 1888

Sigel, Franz, *The Pea Ridge Campaign*, Battles and Leaders of the Civil War, Vol., 1, The Century Company 1887

Snead, Thomas L., *The Conquest of Arkansas*, Battles and Leaders of the Civil War, Vol. 3, The Century Company 1887; *The First Year of the War in Missouri*, Battles and Leaders of the Civil War, Vol. 1, The Century Company 1887

Steele, Phillip, and, Cottrell, Steve, *Civil War in the Ozarks*, Pelican Publishing Company, Gretna, Louisiana 1993

Walker, Wayne T., *Soldiers in War Paint*, The West: True Stories of the Old West magazine, March 1967

Warren, Steve L., *Last Raid at Cabin Creek*, Simitar Entertainment, Inc., Maple Plain, Minnesota 1992

Webb, W.L., *Battles and Biographies of Missourians: Civil War Period of Our State*, Hudson-Kimberly Publishing Company, Kansas City, Missouri 1900

Wherry, William M., *Wilson's Creek, and the Death of Lyon*, Battles and Leaders of the Civil War, Vol. 1, The Century Company 1887

Wilkins, Thurman, *Cherokee Tragedy: The Story of the Ridge Family and the Decimation of a People*, The Macmillan Company, Collier Macmillan LTD., London 1970

Chronology of Battles
and Skirmishes

Wilson's Creek (Oak Hills), Missouri, August 10, 1861
Round Mountain (Red Forks), Oklahoma, November 19, 1861
Bird Creek (Chusto-Talasah), Oklahoma, December 9, 1861
Patriot Hills (Chustenahlah), Oklahoma, December 26, 1861
Pea Ridge (Elkhorn Tavern), Arkansas, March 7-8, 1862
1st Newtonia, Missouri, September 30, 1862
Fort Wayne, Oklahoma, October 22, 1862
Cane Hill, Arkansas, November 28, 1862
1st Cabin Creek, Oklahoma, July 2, 1863
Honey Springs (Elk Creek), Oklahoma, July 17, 1863
Poison Spring, Arkansas, April 18, 1864
Pleasant Bluff (Steamer *J.R. Williams*), Oklahoma, June 15, 1864
Massard Prairie, Arkansas, July 27, 1864
Flat Rock, Oklahoma, September 16, 1864
2nd Cabin Creek, Oklahoma, September 19, 1864

Note: This is only a partial list of the many battles and skirmishes in which Native Americans participated in the War Between the States.

Index

M

Major Ridge 3
Manassas, Virginia 23
Mason-Dixon line 12
Mason, Richard B. 52
Matthews, A.C. 13
Mayes, Joel 21
Maysville, Arkansas 13, 49, 52
McCulloch, Ben 19, 20, 25, 38, 41, 42
McIntosh, D.N. 31, 58
McIntosh, James 32, 33, 34, 40
Mooney, James 6

N

Neosho, Missouri 45
New Echota 2, 11, 12
Newtonia, Missouri 13, 45, 46, 47, 48, 49, 51

O

Oak Hills 12, 27
Old Ridge-Polson Cemetery 14
Old Sacramento 47
Old Telegraph Road 37, 42, 43
Oliver's Prairie 45
Opothle Yahola 29
Opothleyoholo 29, 30, 31, 32, 33, 34

P

Park Hill, Indian Territory 11
Patriot Hills 33, 34
Pea Ridge, Arkansas 12, 37, 39, 40, 41, 43, 45, 48, 49, 51
Pensacola, Oklahoma 69
Pike, Albert 10, 14, 29, 37, 38, 39, 40, 52
Pin Indians 14, 47
Poison Spring 59, 61, 62, 63, 64, 65
Price, Sterling 12, 21, 24, 25, 38, 45, 61, 68

Q

Quayle, Lieut. Col. 30, 32

R

Rains, James S. 52
Ray, John A. 27
Rector, Henry M. 18
Red Fork 30
Red River Campaign 64
Rentiesville, Oklahoma 59
Ridge, John 11
Ridge, Major 3, 4, 11, 12
Ritchey, Matthew H. 46, 48, 49
Ritchey, Missouri 46
Ross, Elizabeth 10
Ross, John 4, 9, 10, 12, 14, 18, 19, 20, 21, 22
Ross' Landing 5

Ross, Quate Martin 10
Round Mountain 30

S

Salomon, Frederick 46, 48
San Jacinto 41
Sarcoxie, Missouri 48
Scott, Winfield 4, 5, 9
Shelby, Joseph O. 46
Sigel, Franz 25, 26, 38, 39, 42
Snead, Thomas L. 21, 25
Southwest City, Missouri 12, 14
Springfield, Missouri 10, 21, 24, 26
Steele, Frederick 61
St. Louis, Missouri 38
Sturgis, Samuel 26
Sugar Creek Hollow 37
Sugar Creek Valley 38
Sweeney, Gen. 26

T

Tahlequah 14, 21
Telegraph Road 37, 42, 43
Texas Military Road 57
Trail of Tears 37
Tulsa, Oklahoma 31
Tulsey Town 31
Tustenuggee, Chief Halek 33

V

Verdigris River 32

W

Walker, Tandy 47, 57, 62, 63
Walnut Creek, Kansas 34
Washburn, Missouri 38
Watie, Stand 12, 13, 14, 40, 43, 53, 57, 59, 67, 68, 69, 70, 71
Watts, Oklahoma 52
Wayne, "Mad" Anthony 52
Wilson's Creek 12, 21, 22, 24, 25, 26, 27, 45
Wool, Gen. 2
Wounded Knee 17

Y

Yale, Oklahoma 30